T0021839

THE 7 CHAKRA CRYSTALS

The 7 Chakra Crystals: A Guide to Find Your Balance and Peace
copyright © 2023 by White Star s.r.l. All rights reserved. Printed in China.
No part of this book may be used or reproduced in any manner whatsoever without
written permission except in the case of reprints in the context of reviews.

Andrews McMeel Publishing
a division of Andrews McMeel Universal
1130 Walnut Street, Kansas City, Missouri 64106

www.andrewsmcmeel.com

First published in 2023 by White Star s.r.l.

Vivida® is a trademark property of White Star s.r.l.
www.vividabooks.com
©2023 White Star s.r.l.
Piazzale Luigi Cadorna, 6
20123 Milan, Italy
www.whitestar.it

23 24 25 26 27 SDB 10 9 8 7 6 5 4 3 2 1

ISBN: 978-1-5248-8125-2

Library of Congress Control Number: 2022948579

Editor: Katie Gould
Designer: Julie Barnes
Production Editor: Dave Shaw
Production Manager: Tamara Haus

ATTENTION: SCHOOLS AND BUSINESSES
Andrews McMeel books are available at quantity discounts with bulk purchase for educational,
business, or sales promotional use. For information, please e-mail the Andrews McMeel
Publishing Special Sales Department: sales@amuniversal.com.

The content of this book is the result of research and studies by the author over the course of 20 years of teaching in his labs and seminars. The use of stones, if done with the correct knowledge, can be valuable for anyone looking for psycho-physical well-being and comprehensive personal growth, offering significant and tangible results.

However, it is important, for an accurate diagnosis, to remember to consult a doctor at the onset or persistence of illnesses or symptoms. Stones are not a replacement for medical treatment, but can offer incredible support.

THE 7 CHAKRA CRYSTALS

A Guide to Find Your Balance and Peace

LUCA APICELLA

Illustrations by

Alessandra De Cristofaro

Andrews McMeel
PUBLISHING®

CONTENTS

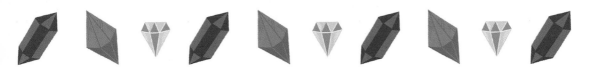

Finding yourself before a rainbow of crystals pleases the eyes and vibrates the soul. And that's not a metaphor! There's a seed of truth to this: stones vibrate, as we do with them.

Maintaining our vibrations is important; but we, unlike crystals, tend to alter or lose our frequency. When a frequency meets a similar frequency, the two align through a small process of compensation. Therefore, we can call stones "our magnificent helpers," which support us in the various moments of our existence, allowing us to restore the lost frequency.

Stones have been a part of the daily life of people since the dawn of time and in every part of the globe, and every great civilization recognized the ritual, magical, symbolic, and aesthetic functions of stones.

In the religious sphere, crystals were assigned various meanings. At the height of society, royal crowns were adorned with precious stones. Some say the purpose of these stones is to increase the connection of the crown chakra (the seventh chakra), aligning it with the requests of the god one aspires to obey.

Stones also had countless uses in the arts and in technical and scientific fields, and still today they continue to be used for many purposes, from more essential to more fun. The arrival of chemical pigments has not replaced natural materials, and often you still find mica used in glitter and eye shadow.

Alongside these uses, ever since antiquity, stones have been used to cure various types of illnesses through what we today call "crystal therapy," a bionatural discipline that has always been a part of complementary medicine.

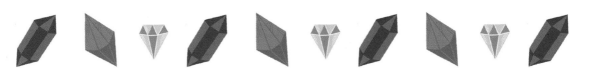

The foundational principle of the discipline consists, in short, of identifying the right stones (including ambers and fossils) that transmit frequencies that help restore unbalanced energy centers through direct or indirect contact. In this sense, the influence of stones is precious to our physical, emotional, mental, and spiritual well-being and supports treatment, from identifying the problem to resolving it.

Naturopathic medicine uses very ancient practices. For example, the medical school of Kos (where the medicine of Hippocrates originated) taught that illness is a consequence of discord between the patient and the elements (earth, water, air, fire) both on the outside and, more importantly, on the inside. The elements are fundamental to moods and organs and, if imbalanced, can cause various disorders. Even back then, the use of stones could restore the so-called "vibrational connection," creating new harmony between the patient and the elements.

We are essentially talking about energy, which if deficient or excessive can be rebalanced by restoring the subtle functioning of the chakras that regulate its use. In other words, it's about reestablishing the balance of our physical or subtle body with the universe and with Mother Nature, which we are a part of, to rediscover our true essence and thus well-being.

There are many types of stones, and each one carries a specific trait to be discovered and studied. Jaspers, agates, quartzes, and many others are all ready to come to our rescue and take us on a journey of awareness that can lead to external and internal growth.

Stones ask us to research and try out crystal therapy, which could help us on many levels.

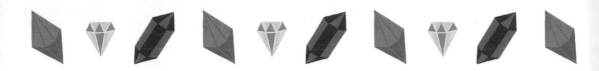

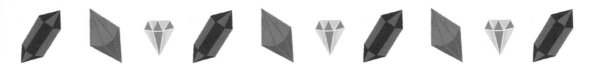

Let's learn how to recognize crystals, learn how to treat them with the right method and clean them appropriately—which sometimes varies from stone to stone. Let's learn how to test them with our hands and with tools like the pendulum and, lastly, to wear them in the right ways and at the right times. We will thus discover which stone is best for us under certain circumstances.

The thirty-seven stones included in this book represent the cornerstone of crystal therapy. We can consider them a starting point, the first independent baby steps in this surprising world, working exclusively on us.

An exciting journey of personal growth that will nurture and grow our being in its entirety is opening up before us. Go on, then! Let's enter the world of stones together.

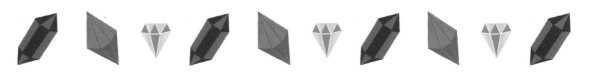

....

CHAPTER 1

WHAT ARE THE 7 CHAKRAS, AND HOW DO THEY WORK?

The word *chakra* comes from Sanskrit and means "circle" or "wheel." According to the tradition of many cultures and religions, chakras are in fact wheels whose energy becomes luminous as they turn. India is the direct heir of Sanskrit culture, which in the most common traditions refers to seven chakras. Upon closer study, the chakras are actually more than forty thousand energy centers, all aimed at managing the fuel that allows our bodies and organs to function. They are cone-shaped, with the apex situated in the spine, and they spin asynchronously. This movement allows the energy to flow without ever stopping, just like breathing. While new energy enters one chakra, another chakra eliminates the old energy, giving it back to the surrounding environment.

Prana, or life energy, is extracted by solar energy and the trees, which on the physical plane are tasked with transforming carbon dioxide into oxygen.

This process happens thanks to specialized chakras, called *etheric chakras,* which are situated outside the physical body and, more specifically, on the auric layers that surround it. Etheric chakras work to collect energy, break it up into six colors, and direct it to the various chakras. Each chakra cone contains six microtubules, each of a different color, that direct the broken-down color from the primary energy toward the chakra of the same color.

The purpose of colors

Each color possesses the vibrational frequency of different electrons. The slowest is red, and the fastest is purple.

This is why the seven chakras have seven different colors: each uses its color to feed the various parts of the body, depending on the frequency it needs.

Proper functioning of the chakras allows energy to flow in a balanced way, feeding the organs in the best way possible. Problems arise when the functioning of the energy centers varies, sending energy to the organs they are connected to in greater or smaller amounts than necessary and thus altering the functioning of the organs, which risk falling ill in the medium term.

That's why it's necessary to keep the energy centers balanced through various useful practices, one of the most important being crystal therapy.

MULADHARA

First Chakra

The first chakra is connected to the element Earth. Here we find all the basic principles essential to our life, such as feeding, sleeping, reproducing, and evacuating. This chakra embodies the principle of survival and multiplication of the species.

Emotions such as aggressiveness take place in Muladhara, which expresses itself through the masculine archetype of the hunter and transformer who, in order to survive, procures food that is then transformed by the feminine in the second chakra. However, do not fall for a trivialized reading of the two principles: masculine and feminine here do not refer to sexual genders, but to the specific characteristics of an individual. The symbolic image is the primitive idea of the male who captures the prey with a spear (active symbolism) and brings it to the cave, where the female receives and transforms it (receptive symbolism). In short, the difference between the two principles—active and receptive—is contained in the first chakra.

The first and fourth chakras are the only ones associated with two colors. More specifically, in the first chakra the color black is associated with managing the state of being rooted, the ability to keep your feet on the ground and face all the practical and emotional tasks that life presents us. On the other hand, the color red is associated with this chakra with regard to the fundamental energy of the physical and subtle organism, such as life force and sex drive.

Even the management of money is tied to Muladhara; spendthrifts, for example, have an imbalance in the first chakra. Hypo- or hyper-sexuality, erection problems, attachment or total detachment from material things, excessive consumption of food, aggressiveness (overt or covert), and "having your head in the clouds" are all associated with the first chakra. Finally, many problems related to the skeletal system are linked to the difficulty of existing, and therefore to the first chakra.

It should be noted that the glands associated with the chakra, ovaries and testicles, fulfill the principle of creation, hence the peculiarity of this chakra.

- **Color:** blood red in activation, black in rooting
- **Location:** the space between the anus and vagina/testicles
- **Harmonizing note:** C
- **Type of action:** masculine, active
- **Body parts affected:** anus and rectum, vulva, vagina, ovaries, part of the uterus, penis, testicles, prostate, skeletal system
- **Glands affected:** gonads
- **Related illnesses:** those related to the genital organs and skeletal system: teeth and nails are also related to the proper functioning of the first chakra
- **Keywords:** "I exist!"

SVADHISTHANA

Second Chakra

Management of our feminine aspects, the skill of introspection, processing of emotions, and listening to yourself are found in the second chakra.

Because emotions are symbolically represented by water, through which they energetically flow, their waste, once processed, is released through urine and feces.

Thanks to Svadhisthana, the animal and primitive nature of reproductive sexuality of the first chakra gives way to emotions and feelings, and the animal being is transformed into a higher being, which associates sexual union with the word "love." The true union of instinct and emotion takes place in this energy point.

In the second chakra, there is a clear perception of one's personal power, which is internalized and manifested through the third chakra at the right time and will become the materialization of what can only be felt up until now.

The diseases related to Svadhisthana have to do with issues related to the processing of emotions and organs related to them, mostly visceral.

The adrenal glands are associated with the second chakra. They produce several hormones, including adrenaline, which activates the crucial phase of fight-or-flight.

- **Color:** bright orange
- **Location:** about two inches below the navel
- **Harmonizing note:** D
- **Type of action:** feminine, receptive
- **Body parts affected:** bladder, kidneys, intestines, lymphatic system

- **Glands affected:** adrenal glands
- **Related illnesses:** those related to organs that treat bodily fluids
- **Keywords:** "I feel!"

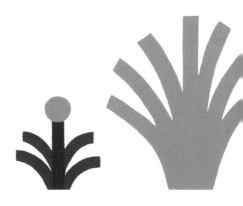

MANIPURA

Third Chakra

The third chakra is connected to the element gold, which in turn is connected to the male principle, characterized by an inclination to being active, and therefore linked to movement, construction, and destruction.

For this reason, Manipura is an expression of personal power that is internalized and processed in the second chakra, Svadhisthana, and then made available as personality to be used in the world.

This energy center gives humans the ability to manifest their power, which is initially internal so that you can achieve personal fulfillment. This power flows from the inside to the outside, manifesting as if it were our fortress: rich, stable, and available to the beauty of life, a warm and powerful sun that radiates through our whole being and those around us, sending a message of power for the good of the whole.

This power aspect can be divided into two parts: on the one hand, the power made available to create projects in the service of others; and on the other, the power to crush others to achieve personal goals. Management of the ego, therefore, becomes crucial. It is positive when we put ourselves at the service of others, whereas it becomes negative when we are faced with an overflowing ego, or when a fragile emotional structure tries to protect itself by crushing others.

The pancreas gland, governed by Manipura, has a very important role because it is responsible for the introjection of affectivity, and therefore of the sweetness that is either produced or absorbed from the outside.

The mismanagement of affection can cause the decompensation of the pancreas and lead to various forms of diabetes, which consist of the initial difficulty and then the inability to process sugar at the cellular level. All this corresponds to the inability to "open to the sweetness" that comes from life.

The third chakra is associated with anxiety (due to fear of the future), depression (fear of acting), and the failure to process the past (fear of evolving), whereas a balanced Manipura is the bearer of vitality so that it can face existence in all its wonderful aspects. Cheerfulness and strength? The perfect mix!

- **Color:** golden yellow
- **Location:** about two inches below the opening of the stomach
- **Harmonizing note:** E
- **Type of action:** masculine, active
- **Body parts affected:** stomach, intestine, liver
- **Glands affected:** pancreas
- **Related illnesses:** those related to organs such as the stomach, intestine, and liver
- **Keywords:** "I am!"

ANAHATA

Fourth Chakra

The fourth chakra is the cornerstone of human existence: love. Human beings are incarnated on Earth to learn to love themselves and the world around them, reaching unconditional feelings as much as possible. It is also the symbol of the freedom to feel, which is connected to a higher will.

There are different types of love: the one Anahata refers to is the fusion of animal love and intellectual love, the cosmic love that puts us on Earth in order to evolve through emotions.

The heart chakra performs two predominant activities: the transformation of human emotions, which are shaped and manifested inside and outside of us; and affectionate support in life's emotionally challenging moments.

Like the first chakra, the fourth is associated with two colors. Emerald green is used when the heart receives an emotion already partially processed by the intestine (second chakra), making it more subtle, and therefore able to be absorbed by every cell in the body, so as to finally allow the human being to change according to the emotion experienced. The heart is in fact a powerful soother, which calms us to allow us to achieve the clarity necessary to deal with problems in case of great trauma or fear.

The color pink instead comes into play when the various events of life destabilize us to the point that we can't react to the stress they cause. It has the power to support us, creating a sort of muffled room we can retreat to. In addition, it modulates the right reaction times, which will then be taken care of through the color green.

The illnesses linked to Anahata have to do with the processing of emotions, which aim to spiritualize a lived experience, that is, to make a change in life based on what has been experienced. A heart attack is a dysfunctional example of this. Lastly, Anahata symbolically asks us to be free and to fly through the lungs.

The related gland is the thymus, which is located about four or five inches below the neck and is responsible for recognizing the best choices for us (good/evil).

- **Color:** emerald green and bright pink
- **Location:** in the middle of the chest, along the nipple line
- **Harmonizing note:** F
- **Type of action:** feminine, transformative

- **Body parts affected:** heart, lungs, circulatory system
- **Glands affected:** thymus
- **Related illnesses:** those of the organs that have to do with the subtle diffusion of emotions
- **Keywords:** "I love!"

VISHUDDHA

Fifth Chakra

The fifth chakra has to do with communication and listening. It has both an external and internal dimension: external when the space outside of us is verbalized, internal when it concerns the ability to listen and communicate the messages coming from the body.

It is recommended to pay close attention to what is said because it might come true. Sometimes a wish is expressed aloud, and the listener is asked not to talk about it to avoid intrusion.

The throat is related to the principle of the word, the vibration. This is the frequency that represents the thought that becomes the word, and therefore, divine manifestation, according to ancient traditions. The fifth chakra has the power to materialize what we think by pronouncing it.

The throat, which houses the vocal cords and speech, frequently has to "swallow a bitter pill," and we often fall ill because of this excess.

The ears, on the other hand, have the ability to listen to what comes from outside, but intuitively also to what comes from within. The illnesses linked to Vishuddha are related to incorrect listening or communication.

A cold or the seasonal flu are signals that we should take some time to stop. As with nature, we need a moment of hibernation to listen to the body, which is sending messages inherent in excessive course of action. We become congested, we stop smelling; our ears become blocked with phlegm; and our throat swells, tired of swallowing uncomfortable things.

The thyroid, the butterfly-shaped gland, symbolically invites us to take flight. It is also the needle on the scale that urges and testifies, through its state of health, the action that favors personal evolution.

Singing the praises of the Lord is equal to singing the praises of one's divine nature, not necessarily in a religious sense.

- **Color:** starry night blue
- **Location:** at the base of the throat
- **Harmonizing note:** G
- **Type of action:** masculine, materializing
- **Body parts affected:** throat, vocal cords, trachea, nose, ears

- **Glands affected:** thyroid gland
- **Related illnesses:** those related to the organs that have to do with communication and listening
- **Keywords:** "I create!"

AJNA

Sixth Chakra

The sixth chakra, or "third eye," with its bright purple color is perhaps the chakra usually attributed with the most importance.

It is the chakra that gives you a clear and sharp vision of your inner self. It allows you to see and perceive the subtle reality around you. It allows us to observe the movement of energy that surrounds us, to see entities and spirit guides, and it offers the possibility to interact with them in a more direct and sometimes more functional way.

It is important to understand, however, that unless the first five chakras are balanced first, Ajna is limited to only marginal function with respect to what we have said.

The sixth chakra is forward-looking. It facilitates the all-around vision of current reality, with the ability to predict events that affect ours and others' lives.

Imagination, clarity, and creativity are part of a well-developed sixth chakra. The more developed Ajna is, the more functional the gifts just mentioned will be.

The illnesses linked to Ajna concern the most common problems with the eyes, such as near-sightedness, which symbolically represents the difficulty of seeing things that life projects from afar, and therefore a lack of foresight. Because we often have to deal with facts that are now very close, urgency is crucial. Likewise, all vision defects send us clear behavioral messages.

In some cases, the use of intellectual faculties is so strong that the individual chooses to stop perceiving emotions in a visceral and profound way, delegating the processing of emotions to the brain—the mental auric layer—which, however, can perform this process only in part and by poorly emulating the gut, the real protagonist of emotional processing.

In these cases, big headaches are expected!

- **Color:** purple
- **Location:** about two inches above the eyebrows
- **Harmonizing note:** A
- **Type of action:** masculine in outer vision and feminine in inner vision
- **Body parts affected:** eyes, central nervous system (brain and spinal cord)
- **Glands affected:** pituitary gland
- **Related illnesses:** those related to the organs that have to do with physical and subtle sight; also problems of the nervous system
- **Keywords:** "I see!"

SAHASRARA

Seventh Chakra

The seventh chakra speaks to us of our connection to the divine dimension, to the universe, which we obey according to precise rules. We start from the assumption that the belief of being totally free is wrong.

Careful listening and observation of the cosmic rules allow us to perceive ourselves as spiritual beings, incarnating a physical body on Earth to experience an evolutionary path. If experiences, whether positive or negative, are absorbed as teachings, they allow us to take steps forward into a deeper understanding of life.

Sahasrara, or the crown chakra, is physically easy to perceive in newborns, who in fact are incarnated on Earth with their fontanelle totally open and totally connected to the cosmic will. Through the fontanelle, one receives nourishment from subtle cosmic energy. From here, by channeling energy through the auric bodies above (the closest ones being causal, mental, astral, or emotional body and etheric double), the brain receives information about its functioning, which will activate or inhibit functions of the body, like illnesses.

The importance of this center lies in the fact that it contains all the work that has been done on the underlying chakras, facilitating a synthesis.

The illnesses linked to the seventh chakra concern the functioning of the psyche; if Sahasrara is somehow "disturbed" by events, it can cause behavioral problems known as psychiatric disorders. Sometimes people with such illnesses feel that their energy is being absorbed by factors foreign to them.

It is also interesting to note that the seventh chakra is often involved in problems related to eating disorders, because any alterations in subtle nourishment are also reflected in the physical one.

The human being, as a spiritual being, needs divine light, and the source ready to receive this nourishment is Sahasrara.

- **Color:** bright white
- **Location:** in the middle of the top of the head, on the fontanelle
- **Harmonizing note:** B
- **Type of action:** feminine
- **Body parts affected:** brain and cerebral cortex
- **Glands affected:** pineal gland
- **Related illnesses:** anorexia, bulimia, and psychiatric disorders
- **Keywords:** "I am connected!"

CHAPTER 2

·················

THE CONNECTION BETWEEN CHAKRAS, ORGANS, AND ILLNESS

The bond between the physical body and the chakra system, or subtle body, at first might seem magical and mysterious; but instead, it should be considered as a set of natural laws that we have ceased to see for some time.

The correct functioning of the chakras requires a healthy physical body. When a problem arises, the cause—and the response—should be sought in the subtle body mechanics, according to which every organ of the body is governed by one or more chakras. Here, a question comes up: If there are seven chakras and many more organs, how does our body work? We should clarify that there are many more chakras than these seven—some count as many as forty-four thousand—and each organ has its main chakra that provides it with energy. Based on this view, there are lots of mini-chakras throughout the body that deal with energy circulation—in other words, the transfer of energy from one part to another or the cleansing of this energy when it becomes too heavy. Being a system in which everything is connected, variations in any of the chakras can cause a reaction in one of the others. Let's find out together why, then, one falls ill.

Emotions

When the energy that comes from the ether and the sun is directed by the chakras to the physical body in a balanced way, it allows the body to use it correctly as fuel.

Asian cultures, through the laws of reincarnation, teach us how every living being—human, animal, plant, and even mineral—chooses to be reincarnated on the Earth in order to fulfill its evolutionary journey. This tradition identifies an evolutionary sequence that starts with minerals and reaches humans before moving to a more subtle, or angelic, form: and from there, it then evolves into increasingly imperceptible forms.

As chance would have it, although it's not really chance, human beings are largely emotional individuals. Just stop for a few minutes and silently listen to yourself, and you'll connect with the emotional waves that pass through you. Even in this very moment, as you read, you feel emotions toward what is written on these pages or what you are experiencing in your personal life: worry, joy, anxiety, excitement, and so on. But what are all these emotions for?

By watching human beings, we see how life develops daily through the use of our five senses (sight, hearing, taste, smell, and touch), which allow us to have purely sensorial experiences that push us to have different reactions.

For example, thanks to our sight, we observe the world with its colors, shapes, and events, whereas through taste we can experience the flavors of life. Touch offers physical pleasure, cold and hot, a caress but also pain. All these sensations lead us to have experiences in a very broad array of emotions, which allow us to enhance various evolutionary tools. We can thus confirm that the senses generate emotions and that emotions are evolutionary impulses.

But do all events and the emotions that accompany them have a specific function for those who feel them? I am led to believe that the response is undoubtedly yes. And this is what makes it even more important to learn to manage individual emotions.

I nurture a worldview that says that whatever the universe throws at me is meant to make me grow. I developed this conviction by living, experiencing, and making mistakes—on some occasions, by getting angry or feeling abused by life.

Over time, with patience, courage, and trust, I noticed that once I understood the message (with the mind) and digested the lesson (in the gut), the same event would never happen again because it had already completed its job, that of allowing me to grow and evolve.

But I have also happened to react excessively, especially at the beginning of my journey, allowing my emotions to get the best of me and damage me emotionally and physically.

What would happen if—when facing the events that life presents us, which are sometimes a great burden—we didn't grasp the message or the lesson? What if we thought the facts of our existence are punishments or chance, or caused by bad luck, that knocks us down as divine retribution? Many people believe that life's events are random and do not consider asking about their causes, but this way of seeing carries a high price to pay.

Illness and its message

Let's try, then, to embrace the idea that every event carries a message that, if understood, can help you in modifying your behaviors. This is what happens if we are trained from a young age to listen.

Socially, in recent centuries we have lost the habit of understanding events, our ability to assign specific meaning to them, and have trusted in the randomness of things. But the messages don't stop coming. On the contrary, they are increasingly frequent, at first subtle and then more explicit, in the hope of being heard and accepted until dysfunctional behaviors are modified.

Eventually the messages—if they remain unheard, based on this interpretation of reality—manifest in the physical body. Manifestations literally reveal themselves, going from a simple cold to more serious illnesses, in order to clearly deliver their message.

The purpose of symptoms

Ever since the arrival of traditional science-based or chemical medicine, starting in the 1940s, the use of chemical medicine to treat symptoms has tended to replace an understanding of symptoms and their slow but deep healing process as a means for curing the illness. Rushed treatment, in any case, will literally smother the precious message that the symptom carries. In the short term the problem will be solved, but the symptom and illness will tend to reappear until the person has received the message. Only then will the illness fulfill its job and disappear "like magic."

What happens in terms of energy? The energy system makes use of an external event to create a sort of disturbance in the subtle body that allows the chakras tied to the affected organ to start functioning more quickly or slowly, depending on the need, varying thus the frequency. In this way, the amount of energy that reaches the organ will be different than usual, which will cause it to malfunction. What we call illness in the West, seen in these terms, appears instead as an alteration in the energy frequency of the organ.

Therefore, let us start to assume the mindset that sees the illness as a message. The energy system will be favored in the process of returning balance; and, where necessary, we will assist it in doing so with therapy that uses the most natural remedies and techniques possible.

What are natural remedies and techniques?

Mother nature is great, and through her many resources (herbs; energy flows: homeopathy, and other remedies like gemmotherapy, magnetic therapy, etc.), she helps people listen to the message until it can reach even the untrained ear.

Among many valid techniques, crystal therapy in particular can be considered effective because by placing the most appropriate stone on the affected spot, it can restore the lost energy frequency to the organ or apparatus in question. Thus, through direct absorption, the frequency of the stone will help the organ return to its harmonious functioning.

This mechanism, in any case, won't be very effective if the carrier hasn't asked the right questions regarding the message that must be understood.

Let us summarize the sequence of events:

- **PREMISE**
  Dysfunctional attitudes ask to be corrected.

- **DEVELOPMENT**
  The universe reveals a message through increasingly intense events.
  The unacknowledged message manifests in the body.
  Choice number one: the human being ignores the message and starts using chemical medicines without facing or resolving the energy causes of the illness.
  Choice number two: the human being tries to understand the message and modifies their dysfunctional behaviors in order to restore balance to their energy.

- **CONCLUSION**
  The illness is able to heal only if it is understood and treated deeply without ignoring its holistic nature.

Let us always remember that the physical body and its energetic bodies are inseparably connected by what the soul, through the experiences of the physical body, wishes to experience in order to evolve.

At this point, I feel the need to highlight one crucial aspect: addressing only one of the parts of a human being, either the physical body or the energetic body, the mind or the emotions, will result in failure.

We must not forget that humans are composed of all these parts and, when even just one of them falls ill, the others also fall ill, in a sort of domino effect. The meaning of the events is the voice of our soul, which is yelling a profound message: it wishes to change in order to get us to evolve.

Only a holistic vision of humans—one that is not made up of separate individual sections—can open the way to a real, healthful, and deep healing process.

THE FREQUENCIES OF OUR BODIES

We know that all of us vibrate at certain frequencies; when these frequencies are high, so is our energy; and thus our body works better, our mood is good, and we become magnets for opportune events. On the contrary, low frequencies cause the body to gradually deteriorate: illnesses appear, and we attract events that we recognize as negative.

Raising frequencies takes constant work; it's an attitude toward life. Careful reflection shows that the stones are successful as treatment and healing because they help restore the original frequency of the body, which inevitably is diminished. Thus, some stones in particular, like angelite, hyaline quartz, and amethyst, can help raise energy frequencies.

Always remember that the stones are our helpers, but if we want to be productive, we must do things, change our lifestyle. Learn to think differently; eat healthful food; sleep at night and live during the day, in the sunlight, so that you can preserve your natural balance.

CHAPTER 3

HOW TO RESTORE HARMONY TO THE CHAKRAS

The physical body and the energetic body are connected and indivisible. It's possible to take care of both by balancing one first and thus also restoring health to the other.

In any case, sometimes after restoring balance it might be necessary to seek a healthy balance between the two poles that will lead to a deep and long-lasting recovery.

The process of restoring balance that starts in the physical body takes longer than it does when it passes from the subtle bodies to the physical body. Therefore, it is suggested to treat both at the same time. There are various acts that can be carried out, and all aim to reestablish the lost frequency.

Positive or negative emotions, which we produce daily, emit frequencies and are always accompanied by a realization of the event that might have caused the possible imbalances.

That's why working simultaneously on the cause and the frequency will allow one or more chakras to rearrange themselves with the right vibration in search of the best equilibrium.

Our body, I repeat, is an integrated and interconnected system that cannot be divided into separate parts.

Chakra 1: Muladhara

Being the chakra that's rooted in the Earth and basic emotions, activities connected to the earth element are important in keeping it in balance, like gardening, being in nature, tribal dances, and sports that help unload aggression like boxing or racket sports.

Sexuality and food, when approached in a balanced way, are of great help to Muladhara.

Red and black stones are recommended for this chakra.

Chakra 2: Svadhisthana

Connection with the water element is particularly important in helping restore Svadhisthana.

Swimming in the sea or a pool helps restore balance to the second chakra. Swimming is the best sport if you need to lose yourself in order to find yourself again. *Watsu* (the combination of water and *shiatsu*) is a treatment that occurs in hot-water tubs and is a true cure-all. With the water temperature at 95°F (35°C), it recalls the place we have felt most protected: the maternal womb.

Listening to and accepting others are also themes connected to this chakra.

Orange stones are best for this chakra.

Chakra 3: Manipura

This chakra wants to express itself in order to expand its inner power. How? By helping your neighbor and taking care of yourself, maybe undertaking new projects. Individual sports develop the third chakra.

Proper handling of the ego activates the right frequency in Manipura, which allows this chakra to recenter itself in relation to an excess or deficiency of personality, dysfunctions that manifest the same vibration and problem.

Yellow stones are recommended for this chakra.

Chakra 4: Anahata

Taking care of your love and tending your inner garden significantly benefit Anahata.

Hugs and dedication to people and planet Earth develop unconditional love, which produces the ideal frequency for bestowing a sense of well-being on this beautiful emerald center.

The best stones for this chakra are green, for use when we want to dissolve the problems tied to the fourth chakra, or pink, when we wish to be supported during our emotional processes.

Chakra 5: Vishuddha

The throat requires external expression. Singing is an important activity. However, we mustn't forget that one of the greatest pains related to Vishuddha is the tendency to not know what to swallow. Thus, meditation and listening to oneself are fundamental. The fifth chakra is also the seat of creation; thus, learning when and how to communicate becomes indispensable to a peaceful life.

Blue stones are recommended for this chakra.

Chakra 6: Ajna

The third eye is known universally for its ability to look inward. Meditation is an important tool of awareness and evolution. Even more useful is contemplation, which helps develop the gifts of clairvoyance, for example, by using a crystal ball, which helps intensely stimulate the Ajna chakra.

Purple stones are best for this chakra.

Chakra 7: Sahasrara

Light is the foundational element of Sahasrara. The connection with celestial planes guarantees balance in this chakra.

Meditation, listening to sacred music, activities that involve the spirit, and prayer are only some of the most effective ways to maintain balance.

White stones—or, better yet, transparent ones—are an excellent vector for connecting with the highest part of ourselves.

PAIRING STONES AND CHAKRAS

I n this book, we have discovered that stones can be advantageous when paired with chakras based on color. This is a good way to improve frequencies.

With time, you will find that it's possible to use stones regardless of color. There are stones, like amethyst and green calcite, that work in very profound ways despite where they are placed, as long as they are used coherently.

Studying is the keyword here, and *feeling* is the crowning element in a search that will over time lead us to become skillful stone users for ourselves and crystal therapists for others. We will then make real "miracles" happen, events that are nothing more than a realization of who we are, what we really want, and finally what we must change in ourselves. In other words, *evolution* is the goal, but *love* is what permits change!

CHAPTER 4

9 STONES FOR OUR CHAKRAS

These nine stones, which I have identified after years of research, if understood and studied well, can prove to be *fundamental stones*, ones that can guarantee strong general support and a high level of effectiveness.

Being familiar with these nine helpers will allow you to treat yourself daily by choosing which stones to keep in your pocket and which to wear. Who, after all, can best listen to the messages of your body and spirit besides you—and thus intervene appropriately?

Similarly, the nine stones can help us through true crystal therapy, which can act on symptoms and guarantee notable and long-lasting results.

The use of these stones is almost as old as the world. They embody the energy we must tap in to when needed in various moments of life.

BLACK ONYX

- **Mineral family:** quartz, chalcedony variety
- **Extraction zones:** Brazil, Mexico, Pakistan
- **Colors:** black, white, yellow, light green
- **Planet:** Venus
- **Sign:** Capricorn

- **Chakra:** first
- **Main purpose:** the strength to do things
- **Musical note:** C
- **Body parts affected:** bones, teeth, legs, feet, skeletal system
- **Keyword:** "Act!"

Black onyx has been known since ancient times. In prehistory, it was used to make common tools, like spearheads that were made of flint, a variety of black onyx.

Where there's onyx, there's obstinacy, stubbornness, the ability to "do what must be done." It can push you to be determined, even when uncomfortable action must be taken.

This stone shows us a unique perspective. Inside black onyx there is a white core that can see and touch our "dark" side (the inner side of us that must evolve), transforming it into a piece of evolved light to be integrated.

In life's more difficult moments, onyx transmits stability and a sense of being rooted in the Earth, allowing us to face even the most emotionally complicated moments.

This stone is effective on the skeletal system, reinforcing it and making it more resistant to breaking. It also has a significant effect on the lower extremities.

INTERESTING DETAIL: In Pakistan, onyx is a light-green/yellow color and transparent. It has been used since antiquity to decorate buildings and make jewelry.

FUN FACT: Each color is used for different energy purposes, from rooting to the Earth (black onyx) to opening up to the bright and spiritual light that comes from above (white onyx).

RED JASPER

- **Mineral family:** quartz
- **Extraction zones:** Turkey
- **Colors:** red, yellow, green
- **Planet:** Mars
- **Sign:** Aries
- **Chakra:** first
- **Main purpose:** the strength to do things
- **Musical note:** C
- **Body parts affected:** blood circulation (especially in the brain)
- **Keyword:** "Act!"

The energy of red jasper promotes a type of basic energy, namely, it allows the body to function in a general sense. It ignites the basic fire needed for energy and emotional circulation to function properly.

"Doing" is the code word for this stone!

We can conform red jasper to fundamental emotions in which the zodiac sign of Aries is recognized for impulsivity and stubbornness, even if sometimes directed in a shortsighted way.

Stubbornness is expressed also through physical resistance, which is another quality of red jasper. Guilt disappears, leaving room for movement that is destined to bring change to our lives.

In short, we can identify this jasper as reawakened fire, which can appropriately shake our life to move us from stagnant situations we are struggling to escape.

It is a powerful protector against energy "vampires," people who have little energy and take it from those around them. Those who are assailed by this type of person endure a sharp drop in energy: loose legs, fatigue, and other similar symptoms. Red jasper is a shield that prevents energy theft.

INTERESTING DETAIL: Jaspers come in different colors. Red is best for protection against energy vampires.

FUN FACT: The only ancient extraction site in all of Europe is in Italy, more specifically in the Lagorara Valley (La Spezia).

CARNELIAN

- **Mineral family:** agate, quartz
- **Extraction zones:** Brazil, Uruguay, Africa
- **Color:** orange
- **Planet:** Mercury
- **Sign:** Virgo
- **Chakra:** second

- **Main purpose:** profound elaboration
- **Musical note:** D
- **Body parts affected:** intestine, liver, ovaries
- **Keyword:** "Feel!"

Carnelian agate is connected to the physical organs that are related to the treatment of water. The organ it affects the most is the intestine. We should always remember that the intestine, on a deep and symbolic level, processes and absorbs emotions. Unexpected emotion, which occurs in moments of high stress, causes many people to "soil themselves" as they run to the toilet. Unexpected defecation comes from high emotional pressure that the intestine can't process and thus seeks to dispel.

Therefore, the use of carnelian is clear: it helps us embrace emotions by allowing us to deeply process them, transforming them into thoughts that don't remain in the mind but are consumed and metabolized and fostering profound change.

The liver draws benefit from it because it helps cleanse the blood to the point of producing the right amount of bile, which is then stored in the gallbladder. There, anger is dosed appropriately for the temperament of the carrier.

For the ovaries, carnelian adjusts menstrual flow and decreases pain.

INTERESTING DETAIL: Be very careful when buying carnelian, and agate in general, because these stones are often tampered with by submerging them in tubs of coloring and exposing them to high temperatures in ovens. This allows for the artificial absorption of the color inside the stone.

FUN FACT: You can most often recognize fake agate from its electric colors, mainly purple, blue, fuchsia, deep black, and aqua green ones.

EMERALD

- **Mineral family:** beryl
- **Extraction zones:** Colombia, Brazil
- **Color:** green
- **Planet:** Venus
- **Sign:** Taurus
- **Chakra:** fourth

- **Main purpose:** love and transformation
- **Musical note:** F
- **Body parts affected:** heart, liver, eyes, lymphatic system
- **Keyword:** "Transform!"

The name of emeralds presumably comes from the Sanskrit word *barag* (flash). This stone is traditionally tied to the magic of love and romanticism. It is often the star of crowns and lavish jewelry, and is found on rings to give your beloved.

Emerald is the queen stone of the heart chakra. Thanks to its action, the fourth energy point can be harmonized to restore balance and activated to reach stabilization.

This wonderful stone is connected to the inner garden, the immense nourishing emotional capacity that the heart possesses by nature. This is a transformative power that can process all the emotions that pass through the energetic heart before cleansing them and then turning them into light energy that can be used. The emotion melts away, and we soon feel lighter.

Emeralds are unique stones—"critical," so to speak, because they require caution in managing them. When placed over someone's heart who possesses sufficient emotional balance, it offers help and compassion to others. However, if the wearer has problems in the management of personal power, it can lead to the overpowering of the weakest in the name of their thirst for domination.

Therefore, emerald should be worn only when we are carefully listening to ourselves, and in any case not for long periods of time, no longer than seven consecutive days.

Two of its principal properties are its anti-inflammatory quality for the liver and its calming action for the eyes.

It can also reharmonize lymphatic circulation and, thus, energy circulation.

INTERESTING DETAIL: Sometimes emeralds are heated in special ovens to make their color more vivid.

FUN FACT: Other stones in the beryl family used for crystal therapy include heliodor, aquamarine, and morganite.

ROSE QUARTZ

- **Mineral family:** quartz
- **Extraction zones:** Brazil, Madagascar
- **Color:** pink
- **Planet:** Venus
- **Sign:** Libra
- **Chakra:** fourth

- **Main purpose:** support in hard times
- **Musical note:** E
- **Body parts affected:** blood pressure, heart function
- **Keyword:** "Treat!"

"Support me, rose quartz, when I am at the mercy of the sea, when life sails on waves that are too high for me, when everything around is dark. Help me to wait for the dawn after this long and cold night, until the warmth of the sun can find the route that's been lost and my heart stops beating like crazy!"

The big task of the rose quartz is enclosed in these few words: support us in the emotionally challenging moments of life in which we aren't able to control our emotions and we need help. Events like mourning, loss, or simply the desire to be consoled find refuge in this quartz.

The heart is nothing more than a great cleanser, which, like a blast furnace, cleans the emotions we feel and then sends them as vehicles of information to all the physical and energetic body.

Blood pressure benefits from rose quartz, especially in cases of hypotension, recalibrating its parameters.

One important thing to note: Because quartz is a very powerful stone, it shouldn't be worn for more than five consecutive days, followed by a five-day break. Using it for longer carries the risk of symptoms like chest heaviness, heart racing, and extra-systole, which in the long term can create more severe problems.

INTERESTING DETAIL: The quality extracted in Madagascar is particularly clear and intense in color.

FUN FACT: Did you know that rose quartz can help with beauty treatments? Place rose quartz in a natural hydrating lotion for at least three days. Massaging the body with the lotion, which will have absorbed the vibrations of the stone, will make the skin smoother and softer.

CITRINE QUARTZ

- **Mineral family:** quartz
- **Extraction zones:** Brazil, Madagascar, USA
- **Color:** yellow
- **Planet:** Sun
- **Sign:** Leo

- **Chakra:** third and spleen
- **Main purpose:** optimism
- **Musical note:** E
- **Body parts affected:** diaphragm, spleen, pancreas, stomach
- **Keyword:** "Positivity!"

Looking at a citrine quartz, especially the lemon variety, the sun immediately comes to mind, with its warmth and brilliance, and also the light at the end of the tunnel in which we may have been stuck for some time.

The attitude of this quartz, and of most yellow stones, is that of the "half-full glass," as it adds optimism to our view of life.

In daily life, things happen that test our stability. Citrine quartz pushes us to find the good in events, reminding us that nothing happens randomly, but instead everything is meant to teach us something. Therefore, in life's events, there's always a lesson to learn to improve ourselves.

Self-esteem benefits from it, and the solar plexus, located two inches below the stomach opening, is harmonized by it, pushing us to believe in ourselves.

The spleen chakra is supported as the body's energy dispenser.

The pancreas, which symbolizes handling the sweetness of life, gets assistance in producing insulin, and therefore the hormone that symbolically allows you to open yourself up to sweetness, receiving it and learning to give it. It improves the functioning of the stomach by calibrating its juices.

INTERESTING DETAIL: There are two types of citrine quartz, a natural and an artificial one, the latter having a bright color and a milky white part, called the "madeira" citrine quartz. It is the most commonly sold. Natural citrine quartz has nice coloring and low availability.

FUN FACT: The "madeira" citrine quartz is actually an amethyst that is heated at high temperatures and changes color from purple to yellow, or even burnt yellow or brown.

SODALITE

- **Mineral family:** quartz
- **Extraction zones:** Brazil, Namibia, Bolivia
- **Color:** blue
- **Planet:** Jupiter
- **Sign:** Sagittarius
- **Chakra:** fifth

- **Main purpose:** mediated communication
- **Musical note:** G
- **Body parts affected:** throat
- **Keywords:** "Think and communicate!"

"If only I could calmly communicate this anger I feel inside that afflicts my mind and leaves me breathless. If only I could find peace in these gritted teeth and clenched jaw like a dog making a feast of its prey. . . ."

Sodalite brings its intense blue to calm furious rage, offering us the key to expressing it in a productive and nondestructive way and pushing us to reflect.

It can help transform aggression into glorified communication, communication that taps into our wise and profound side.

It stimulates the functioning of the throat chakra located in the back at the base of the neck, which oversees insights, helping us recognize and then fully understand how to resolve the problem in question.

Communication in general benefits from it in a very functional way.

The throat and vocal cords are supported by this stone.

Sodalite is highly recommended for singing, and especially sacred singing, making it more inspired and connected to the celestial spheres.

INTERESTING DETAIL: The blue color is intertwined with white for a more spiritual communication.

FUN FACT: Sodalite was used by Native American people to better direct anger.

AMETHYST

- **Mineral family:** quartz
- **Extraction zones:** Brazil, Uruguay, Africa
- **Color:** purple
- **Planet:** Jupiter
- **Sign:** Sagittarius
- **Chakra:** sixth
- **Main purpose:** clarity
- **Musical note:** A
- **Body parts affected:** nervous system, innervation
- **Keyword:** "See!"

When we think about amethyst, its purple color is what first comes to mind. Because it's precisely the mind that we turn to when we need clarity about something.

In reality, the reference comes before the mind since it is a quartz that points to the spiritualization of reality, thus the soul. It teaches us that what we see is almost never as it seems, that behind every fact of life is an evolutionary explanation.

The third eye, or the sixth energy point, located two inches above the eyebrows, benefits significantly from amethyst, which helps emphasize sight, hearing, and subtle sensations in general.

It is excellent for the nervous system, helping calm annoying headaches.

Dream activity is enhanced, and the stone helps remember dreams and find the message offered for evolutionary purposes.

In general, stones shouldn't be used in the bedroom, with the exception of amethyst. Like always, however, temporary use is best, as needed and not out of habit.

It's good to remember that stones tend to stimulate subtle bodies in their profound work at night, which can thus make sleep less restorative.

INTERESTING DETAIL: Amethyst can be naturally mixed with citrine quartz, producing a purple-and-yellow stone called an ametrine quartz.

FUN FACT: Exposing amethyst to high temperatures transforms it from purple to yellow, creating "madeira" citrine quartz with a more accessible price than authentic citrine quartz.

HYALINE QUARTZ
(ROCK CRYSTAL)

- **Mineral family:** quartz
- **Extraction zones:** Brazil, Madagascar, Italy
- **Color:** transparent
- **Planet:** all
- **Sign:** all
- **Chakra:** seventh

- **Main purpose:** increase vibration frequencies
- **Musical note:** B
- **Body parts affected:** nervous system
- **Keyword:** "Connect!"

When I think about hyaline quartz, my mind goes to the powerful, clear, and bright druzes that made the city of Atlantis work. In fact, rock crystal possesses a very high frequency that can amplify the message it is invested in around it.

This crystal naturally has a single tip (single termination) or double tip (double termination). With these crystals, we can amplify our own frequencies by raising them up and helping us overcome various dysfunctional behavioral issues by first understanding them.

It can be used throughout the body and is particularly effective on the seventh chakra, the center of our connection with our spiritual side.

It is possible to use hyaline quartz as a "laser" to cleanse environments and subtle bodies, in addition to its many uses for empowerment and expansion of consciousness. For these more complicated techniques, however, it is important to seek assistance from experienced people who know how to use such powerful tools and avoid potential harm. The nervous system is well served by this crystal, stimulating it for healing purposes.

INTERESTING DETAIL: Quartz is used in digital devices, like quartz watches, because it provides a constant oscillating frequency that keeps precise time.

FUN FACT: Hyaline quartz is also called rock crystal. The first is the scientific name and the second is the common name, which recalls its glass-like transparency.

....

28 STONES FOR PSYCHO-PHYSICAL WELL-BEING

This selection of stones from the hundreds available is a collection of other interesting *helpers*, in addition to the nine fundamental stones already mentioned, as assistance for more specific personal needs. With these twenty-eight stones, precise themes are addressed at the right depth.

To know the crystals better, you must first study them and then handle them directly to fully get a feel for them. I suggest keeping them in your hand or setting them on a specific area of the body for a few minutes, and then listening carefully to the physical, mental, and spiritual reactions they elicit. You must be ready to embrace the effects they have on energy, which sometimes can be very subtle and in other cases are more obvious and explicit.

BLACK TOURMALINE

- **Mineral family:** silicates
- **Extraction zones:** Brazil, China
- **Color:** black
- **Planet:** Saturn
- **Sign:** Capricorn
- **Chakra:** first
- **Main purpose:** absorption
- **Musical note:** C
- **Body parts affected:** bones, teeth, legs, feet, skeletal system
- **Keyword:** "Cleanse!"

Black tourmaline is an elongated and grooved crystal. Stones with such a structure are effective for absorption and drainage of some types of energy.

The potential of this stone is expressed toward electromagnetic energy, which is absorbed and in part drained away by electronic devices in general.

We are surrounded by appliances that work with electric energy and emit electromagnetic charges, dirtying the surrounding environment to the point of damaging those who live there. Washers, microwaves, air conditioners, computers (especially screens), and other devices create electromagnetic fields that alter the biological functions of the body, disrupting the frequencies of the physical organs that are already weak. There are many different effects: chronic fatigue, headache, vomiting, head-spinning, rashes, and other obvious symptoms. In the long term, these symptoms become debilitating and are resolved only by eliminating the sources and driving them away.

A "friendly remedy" might be black tourmaline, which, if placed near appliances, can absorb their electromagnetic charge and decrease the dirty environmental energy. Black tourmaline, however, can do little for antennas and 4G and 5G Wi-Fi routers that radiate nonfilterable electromagnetic frequencies.

Black tourmaline is effective in rooting to the Earth when one is going through a difficult moment or managing intense events. Lastly, it benefits conductivity in innervations of the spine and the elasticity of the ribcage.

INTERESTING DETAIL: Tourmalines have different colors that range from black to red, yellow, green, pink, blue, white, and even multicolor.

FUN FACT: There is a wonderful red and green tourmaline that is used in crystal therapy called watermelon tourmaline.

BLACK OBSIDIAN

- **Mineral family:** volcanic glass
- **Extraction zones:** all over the world
- **Color:** black
- **Planet:** Saturn
- **Sign:** Capricorn

- **Chakra:** first
- **Main purpose:** explosive strength
- **Musical note:** C
- **Body parts affected:** skeletal system, peripheral circulation
- **Keyword:** "Explode!"

Speaking of obsidian as a stone is not quite correct. In reality, it is a natural glass formed by volcanic gas. It is strong in contacting the emotions that we have concealed from our conscious side—which, however, continue to manifest through physical and emotional symptoms—until we see them and bring them to our awareness so that we can process and absorb them.

Like a volcano, obsidian promotes the reemergence of such emotions in a powerful way so that we can transform them from the dark and ambiguous side to the bright and evolved side, which can make us continue from wherever we were held back.

Obsidian is a means for learning to know yourself by bringing to light your personality, which often does not walk in line with your soul but drives you to experiences that diverge from it.

It promotes rooting in those people who struggle to keep their feet on the ground, anchored to reality, preferring an attitude inclined to instability and levity, like a butterfly.

Black obsidian is interesting for its abilities to reunite the more fragile areas of the bones and benefit peripheral circulation.

INTERESTING DETAIL: There are different types of obsidian depending on elements in the gas that creates it. For example: rainbow (iris), sheen, and snowflake.

FUN FACT: Where can you find obsidian? Wherever there's a volcano, there's obsidian.

GARNET

- **Mineral family:** nesosilicates
- **Extraction zones:** India, Madagascar, Sri Lanka
- **Color:** red
- **Planet:** Pluto
- **Sign:** Scorpio
- **Chakra:** first
- **Main purpose:** energy activation
- **Musical note:** C
- **Body parts affected:** circulatory system, adrenal glands
- **Keyword:** "Energy!"

At first glance, garnet can appear almost black and opaque. However, placing it in the light will make it shine! Its famous red glows, warming the eyes and hearts.

And yes, garnet is a producer of heat and thus fire in large quantities. Wearing a garnet means reloading yourself with ready-to-use energy, increasing the basic fire of life. When we are very tired and feel like we have no more energy, garnet is ready to stimulate the adrenal glands, producing cortisol and reserve energy.

It was fashionable during World War I in Italy, used as a parure of rings, necklaces, and earrings. It was used to give strength, the strength to carry on, despite all the adversities of that period.

The beautiful garnet is a stone suitable for moments when energy is scarce, or we think we cannot cope with yet another difficult situation. It is the joie de vivre that manifests in the physical body.

In crystal therapy, it is the ace up the sleeve: for example, during a reading of the chakras, it shows where there is turmoil or helps identify the chakras in question.

It is effective in raising blood pressure and is an important activator of the adrenal glands. It is therefore in general an activator of the physical body.

INTERESTING DETAIL: Garnet should not be worn for prolonged periods, no more than fifteen days followed by a break of four days. This is to avoid both overloading the energy system and subsequent problems it might cause on the physical body.

FUN FACT: When mixed with fine sand, garnet can be used with a waterjet tool to cut steel and other hard materials.

RUBY

- **Mineral family:** aluminum oxide
- **Extraction zones:** Burma, Madagascar, China
- **Color:** red
- **Planet:** Pluto
- **Sign:** Scorpio
- **Chakra:** first
- **Main purpose:** activation
- **Musical note:** C
- **Body parts affected:** genitals, adrenal glands
- **Keyword:** "Passion!"

Ruby is used in crystal therapy as an activator of basic energy, with an important focus on sexual energy. It activates the libido, especially male but also female.

Like all red stones, it affects one's fundamental nature, which refers to the basic emotions related to food (hunger), reproduction (sex), and survival (aggression).

It stimulates the first chakra, increasing physical, emotional, and mental energy.

Where there once was pessimism, now life is full of new goals to be achieved with joy and the drive to do things.

A ruby placed on the first chakra activates sexual energy by pushing us to the act of mere reproduction.

A ruby placed on the heart teaches us something new about sex, the possibility of doing it with feeling and entering the sphere of love.

It also works well on the final part of the intestine, helping to release inflammation that affects the entire organ. It is also valid for erection problems, especially if caused by mental issues.

INTERESTING DETAIL: The most sought-after ruby type is called "pigeon blood" because it is deep red in color with blue reflections.

FUN FACT: There is a variety called "star ruby" for the unique refraction of light on the front that looks like a bright star.

ORANGE CALCITE

- **Mineral family:** calcium carbonate
- **Extraction zones:** different areas of the world, especially in Mexico
- **Color:** orange
- **Planet:** Mercury
- **Sign:** Virgo
- **Chakra:** second
- **Main purpose:** flow of emotions
- **Musical note:** D
- **Body parts affected:** intestine, prostate
- **Keyword:** "Elaborate!"

The orange color of this calcite is beautiful, intense, and very warm. It acts on the second chakra, which is softened when it is subjected to considerable stress or to trauma of great impact.

They say that the intestine is our second brain. In my opinion, it is the first because it is more visceral and especially emotional. The emotional sphere cannot be accepted or assisted by the brain, which instead deals only with the functioning of the body.

A problematic second chakra tends to send the third one off its axis. Orange calcite helps awaken the second chakra, thus aligning also the third one, which will manage externally what has been processed and introjected by the second one.

Like all calcites, the orange variety helps lower noise and upset in the mind to make room for balanced emotions.

The body benefits from calcite in the bones in general. The organs of the lower abdomen benefit from the use of calcite as a softening and therefore relaxing tonic.

INTERESTING DETAIL: Calcite comes in different colors: red, orange, yellow, green, pink, blue, and white.

FUN FACT: Calcite is found all over the world. In caves, it is clearly visible through stalactites and stalagmites, large calcite concretions resulting from the slow sedimentation of water drops.

SUNSTONE

- **Mineral family:** feldspar
- **Extraction zones:** Norway, India
- **Color:** orange
- **Planet:** Mercury
- **Sign:** Gemini
- **Chakra:** second and third

- **Main purpose:** optimism
- **Musical notes:** D, E
- **Body parts affected:** intestine, nerves and muscles, stomach
- **Keywords:** "The glass is half full!"

Sunstone, with its golden reflections, is reminiscent of the star it gets its name from. It is an interesting bridge between the two energy points of the second and third chakras; it brings openness and sunshine. It pushes the second chakra to open the personal, internalized power located in the bowels, and therefore is more masculine. It also invites us to bloom, moving this energy to the third chakra to reveal it to the world, transforming the personal power into power for the benefit of the community.

Thanks to this stone, the second energy point is favored when it is difficult to express oneself in the world due to being stuck in emotions, in the waters of the unconscious, which do not allow evolution. This creates a tendency to close oneself off in a so-called ivory tower, sometimes in search of solitude.

The channels that carry energy from the lower part of the body to the upper part benefit from this stone, as it restores balance to the flow.

It is effective for nonchronic depression. It activates nerves and muscles in times of crisis without creating additional stress. It does a good job of aiding in the functioning of the stomach.

INTERESTING DETAIL: Due to the rarity of the most beautiful and luminous variety, sunstone is sometimes counterfeited in a version that uses plastic and glass substances, creating a myriad of bright dots that have nothing to do with the authentic item.

FUN FACT: Sunstone embodies masculine energy and is the complement of moonstone, which embodies feminine energy.

CHIASTOLITE ANDALUSITE

- **Mineral family:** nesosilicate
- **Extraction zones:** Spain, France, USA, Australia
- **Color:** brown
- **Planet:** Saturn
- **Sign:** Capricorn

- **Chakra:** second
- **Main purpose:** protection
- **Musical note:** D
- **Body parts affected:** bones, venous system
- **Keywords:** "I protect you!"

Chiastolite is just a variety of andalusite. At first glance, it makes an immediate impression due to its unique rhombic shape with a cross in the center.

It is used for protection, especially when there is strong disharmonic energy to be addressed, to prevent it from damaging the people it comes into contact with.

It is recommended for operators and therapists who work with people and want to shield themselves from their strong energy, especially in work involving the energy of the Earth.

It stimulates awareness of facts and situations that act in the dark and that we cannot or do not want to see.

It particularly benefits the solar plexus (the third chakra), which also physically helps us relax at times when anxiety is very high. This chakra is also effective in helping contract the opening of the stomach.

Chiastolite andalusite has strong effects on the psychological and physical structure, strengthening them, stabilizing people who are emotionally distressed, and performing excellent work on the lower limbs.

INTERESTING DETAIL: For protection, since it is a very dense stone, it should be worn for only short intervals of time and not abused, because it tends to lower the frequencies of the body to be protected.

FUN FACT: One of the first extraction sites was found in Spain, near Santiago de Compostela. The sacred path and the stone were immediately related as protectors of the Christian religion.

PETRIFIED WOOD
(FOSSIL WOOD)

- **Mineral family:** fossil
- **Extraction zones:** USA, Balkans
- **Color:** brown
- **Planet:** Mercury
- **Sign:** Virgo
- **Chakra:** second

- **Main purpose:** stability
- **Musical note:** D
- **Body parts affected:** bones and joints, cysts
- **Keyword:** "Melt!"

Speaking about petrified wood as a stone is not accurate; it is technically a fossil. Over time, natural events such as volcanic eruptions knocked down trees that were then buried. In the absence of oxygen, the buried plant did not decompose, leaving room for elements like quartz, keeping the structure intact in appearance but totally changing it on a chemical level.

The first important property of petrified wood is its ability to root to the Earth people who tend to be unstable, unable to face the challenges life presents, sometimes even daily. There are a number of root stones, and this is one of the most powerful.

Petrified wood helps us perform the most challenging actions by finding the right energy.

One interesting quality is that when it is paired with azurite, it affects regressions to past lives. Together these two stones can lift the veil that prevents our present incarnation from seeing previous lives, giving us the possibility to embrace some characteristics we might have inherited and to understand the reason behind certain attitudes, fears, and traumas that might seem devoid of logical reason.

It tends to loosen the bones and joints of people who are excessively rational and prone to mental and physical rigidity.

Research and experiments have been carried out that specifically concern cysts. During examination, the use of petrified wood has shown a significant acceleration in the regression of the problem.

INTERESTING DETAIL: It is a very strong stone, not recommended for people who are physically weak, and therefore have a poor attitude toward being rooted, as it could cause strong disturbances for them.

FUN FACT: There are many sites in the world where you can see entire petrified forests.

PYRITE

- **Mineral family:** iron sulfide
- **Extraction zones:** Peru, Italy, USA
- **Color:** yellow
- **Planet:** Mercury
- **Sign:** Gemini
- **Chakra:** third
- **Main purpose:** exposing fear
- **Musical note:** E
- **Body parts affected:** bones, joints
- **Keywords:** "I understand!"

Pyrite is probably one of the most commonly chosen stones by kids and adults alike. You want it for its color, which resembles gold; you want it for the light it emanates; but you want it especially because it exposes the cause of that discomfort you feel but cannot understand, that unease that makes you live as if you were adrift waiting for something to happen.

If you wear pyrite, the answer will come suddenly in the form of a thought, an event, an encounter. In short, life will offer the answer, making you sigh a breath of relief and say "Now I get it!"

It simply makes us notice the reason, without any emotional involvement; it just shows us the cause.

It is an excellent drainer of bodily fluids that contain the emotions we must now let go of. It increases the fire element, making you more reactive.

On a physical level, it helps you understand the deeper message of a symptom, something psychosomatic that, once understood and acted upon, then allows the issue to stop and sometimes to reverse.

INTERESTING DETAIL: It is a very strong stone, not recommended for people who are physically weak and therefore have a poor grounding, as it could cause strong disturbances for them.

FUN FACT: The word *pyrite* derives from the Greek word *pyr*, meaning "fire." It has been known since ancient times that if this stone is struck with another pyrite or metal, it emits sparks, starting a fire. It thus earned the name of fire stone, or flint.

TIGER'S EYE

- **Mineral family:** quartz
- **Extraction zones:** South Africa
- **Color:** yellow
- **Planet:** Mercury
- **Sign:** Gemini

- **Chakra:** third
- **Main purpose:** perfectionism
- **Musical note:** E
- **Body part affected:** abdomen
- **Keyword:** "Observe!"

Speaking of tiger's eye, we immediately think of its gold-colored reflections. It is actually a powerful quartz that enhances focus on the details of a situation. Therefore, it is a highly recommended stone in circumstances in which a high level of attention is required and in which a detail could make all the difference.

It boosts self-esteem, increasing self-confidence. Joy thus takes hold, bestowing greater lightness and the courage to face events in which one hesitates.

It is an interesting stone of protection that fully addresses the physical side, helping to protect oneself from unexpected events. The diaphragm increases the capacity for movement, thus allowing a greater expansion of the lungs and a greater absorption of oxygen. The functioning of the liver and pancreas derive benefits.

INTERESTING DETAIL: The reflections of the tiger's eye produces an optical effect called "chatoyancy," typical also of some other stones such as hawk's eye and bull's eye.

FUN FACT: The ancient Romans used tiger's eye to protect themselves from wounds in war. In the Middle Ages, it was a means of protection against spells and demons.

YELLOW AND HONEY CALCITE

- **Mineral family:** calcium carbonate
- **Extraction zones:** different areas of the world, especially in Mexico
- **Color:** yellow
- **Planet:** Mercury
- **Sign:** Leo
- **Chakra:** third
- **Main purpose:** tranquilizing
- **Musical note:** E
- **Body parts affected:** diaphragm and stomach, bones, connective tissues
- **Keywords:** "I will shine!"

In thinking about yellow calcite, our attention is immediately drawn to one of the biggest problems of the twentieth century onward: anxiety. The third energy center is precisely the area where anxiety is somatized and associated with the fear of future events. This calcite in particular is good at calming the mind that generates anxiety, and bestowing the lucidity and tranquility needed to act and thus prevent the anxiety from devouring us.

Calcite also does an excellent job on injuries and the disintegration of our aura that arises due to surgery or verbal arguments.

Confusion tends to subside, allowing us to find a quick solution to problems.

Tensions in the physical, mental, and spiritual body diminish, and sleep increases its restorative function.

The so-called honey or amber variety is more transparent and glossier. It becomes the stone of the superego, which helps us to embark on important paths, pushing us toward the completion of projects that we would have considered impossible shortly before.

The honey color infuses light and warmth and can give us the strength to act. It is effective on gastric juices, helping to prevent reflux. It relaxes the diaphragm. It carries out important work on the bone structure in general and on connective tissues.

INTERESTING DETAIL: The diaphragm, symbolically, is called the organ of life and death because it allows the lungs to take in air. Amber calcite allows the diaphragm to function well.

FUN FACT: A variety of calcite which is very light yellow in color is also found in Italy.

YELLOW FLUORITE

- **Mineral family:** halide
- **Extraction zones:** Argentina
- **Color:** yellow
- **Planet:** Mercury
- **Sign:** Gemini
- **Chakra:** third
- **Main purpose:** balancing
- **Musical note:** E
- **Body parts affected:** liver and intestine
- **Keywords:** "I feel!"

Yellow fluorite, similarly to the whole family of different-colored fluorites, is lined with shades of green or brown. Contrasting it with the light, it is as if the yellow color, representing the mental aspect, is pierced by the green, the reigning color of the heart chakra.

This stone is useful for people who tend to analyze daily events in a cold and rational way. It helps them to enter a mode of emotional listening in which a frozen mind, which is meant to protect the person from excessively strong events, gives way to the heart.

The heart, by nature, tends to melt the ice, creating the right warmth to allow the person to live their emotional side to the fullest and then transmit these emotions to the second chakra, which will digest them, metabolize them, and eliminate the waste that's no longer needed.

Yellow fluorite is particularly suitable for those who face life in a logical way—mainly using the left side of the brain—without considering that perhaps there is another more creative and welcoming way that allows you to find more imaginative but also functional solutions, using the right side of the brain.

It is an excellent stone for helping us get in touch with our feminine side, which is receptive and sensitive, but sometimes submerged in the directive and linear masculine side.

It also works well on the liver, helping it to switch the way it makes decisions in favor of the more creative way.

In times of stagnation, the intestine benefits from it.

Bones and teeth are fortified by the fluorine it contains.

INTERESTING DETAIL: Yellow fluorite is useful for learning, and it keeps the mental side balanced with the emotional side.

FUN FACT: Fluorite comes in wide range of colors: yellow, pink, green, blue, purple, and white.

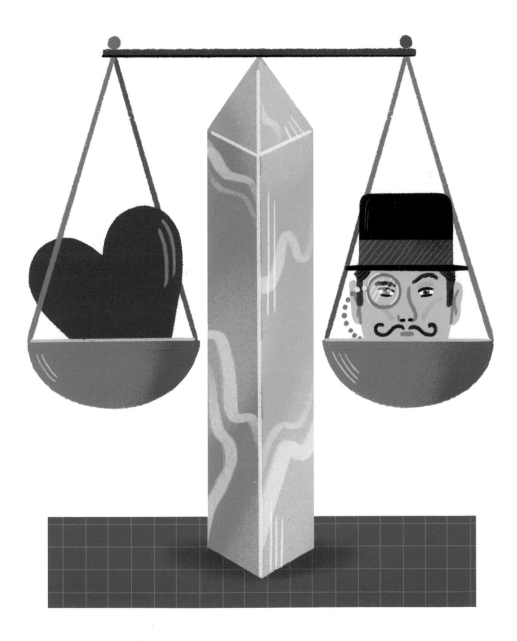

GREEN AVENTURINE

- **Mineral family:** chalcedony quartz
- **Extraction zones:** Brazil, Russia, China, India
- **Color:** green
- **Planet:** Venus
- **Sign:** Taurus
- **Chakra:** fourth
- **Main purpose:** cleansing
- **Musical note:** F
- **Body parts affected:** heart, arteries
- **Keyword:** "Free!"

Green aventurine gets its name from the specks of mica in it, which make it shine.

It is excellent for the physical heart if there are fatty deposits, or atheromas, that impede the passage of blood to the heart and damage it. We can compare these fat deposits to emotions that we are unable or unwilling to let dissolve by the heart chakra in order to be circulated and processed.

Green aventurine helps melt emotions and let go of old patterns that are no longer needed.

Being a green-colored stone, it promotes the processing of emotions in general, prompting proper functioning of the heart chakra. This quartz helps us focus on the fact that the heart is the center of everything, and that love can melt away any fears or problems. It reminds us that our actions toward others can, sooner or later, affect us.

It is a good anti-inflammatory and an excellent tonic for the body.

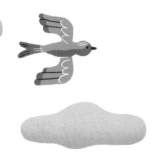

INTERESTING DETAIL: The reflections generated by the pieces of mica contained in aventurine give this stone its "aventurescence" characterized by the presence of golden glares. It was believed that mica was present by chance (or *aventura*).

FUN FACT: Aventurine exists in green, red, brown, and yellow colors. Sunstone is a member of the aventurine family.

MALACHITE

- **Mineral family:** carbonate
- **Extraction zones:** Africa
- **Color:** green
- **Planet:** Venus
- **Sign:** Taurus

- **Chakra:** fourth
- **Main purpose:** anti-inflammatory
- **Musical note:** F
- **Body part affected:** liver
- **Keyword:** "Beauty!"

Malachite is a stone linked to femininity. It brings beauty and sensuality with its round and harmonious shapes. In fact, it harmonizes the feminine side and strengthens it. It has multiple actions.

It helps process emotions, favors the gradual re-emergence of trauma, especially in the sexual sphere at a young age.

It inclines one to the main trait of the feminine principle: welcoming. It favors the relaxation of the body, especially with respect to anger. It is a powerful anti-inflammatory and works on the absorption of inflammation of the body. Thanks to its high copper content, it fights menstrual pain, also helping the regulation of the menstrual cycle. It also effects the fluidization of bile carried from the liver to the gallbladder.

There are many beliefs about the power of malachite: for example, the Spanish phrase *quita-el-mal* meant it was believed that malachite could be a powerful protector from negative energies.

It is undoubtedly a highly absorbent stone, which needs to be cleansed frequently, more than the others, as it could release the low energy it has absorbed. Be careful when placing malachite in direct contact with the skin because, especially in summer, it can leave a toxic copper-green substance that stains the skin.

INTERESTING DETAIL: In ancient times, pulverized malachite was used by artists to obtain the color green.

FUN FACT: It is considered the stone of midwives because it stimulates the contractions of childbirth.

RHODOCHROSITE

- **Mineral family:** carbonate
- **Extraction zones:** Argentina, China
- **Color:** pink
- **Planet:** Venus
- **Sign:** Libra
- **Chakra:** fourth

- **Main purpose:** releasing
- **Musical note:** F
- **Body parts affected:** heart, tissues
- **Keywords:** "Space for the new!"

Rhodochrosite is a difficult stone to manage. It helps when the emotions in the heart chakra are stagnant and you need to let them go.

Rhodochrosite is a very powerful stone, forcing us to let emotions go at all costs, by hook or by crook.

Rhodochrosite pushes us out of our comfort zone so that new emotions can arise to be felt and lived. It leads to confrontation so that our truth and love may surface. It does this in a powerful way, regardless of who is in front of us. This happens because rhodochrosite asks us to love ourselves instead of constantly mediating with the people around us, and does not allow this lesson to be put off.

It pushes us to see the beauty of life in a deeper way, digging into the more spiritual part.

It works on deep cellular regeneration; it softens and regenerates the pericardium, the membrane that lines the heart.

In addition to healing the skin and lungs, particularly the mucous membranes of the bronchi, it helps regenerate bone marrow.

INTERESTING DETAIL: The name rhodochrosite comes from two Greek words: *rhodon*, meaning pink, and *chromos*, meaning color. It is the national stone of Argentina, where the most beautiful deposits ever discovered are found.

FUN FACT: It is considered the stone of the Incas; an Andean legend says that in the center of one of the mountains of Peru, there is an enormous heart of rhodochrosite.

LEPIDOLITE
(PINK MICA)

- **Mineral family:** trioctahedral mica
- **Extraction zones:** USA, Russia
- **Color:** pink-purple
- **Planet:** Venus
- **Sign:** Libra
- **Chakra:** fourth, sixth

- **Main purpose:** calming
- **Musical note:** F
- **Body parts affected:** heart, tissues, nervous system
- **Keyword:** "Rest!"

Pink mica is fascinating. It comes in many layers, and with a little care you can even separate them; in doing so, you'll find that it's extremely light, often semitransparent.

It is applied in two main areas: the heart and the brain, from which it can reach the entire nervous system.

The heart particularly benefits when irregular beats indicate that the fourth chakra is making an effort, often for the purpose of processing one or more emotions that are difficult to metabolize. The heart tries to dissolve these hostile emotions with the additional beats. Obviously, we are referring to episodes that are sporadic and due to emotional disorders.

It is a stone that tends to calm the entire nervous system and allows you to maintain a connection with your intuitions, which thus access their maximum potential.

The nervous system benefits when some psychiatric disorders are present, in which mood stabilizers and lithium are necessary internally. When stability is fluctuating but not chronically, lepidolite helps stabilize the mood.

It calms agitation and, in cases of disturbed sleep, allows for a restorative night.

INTERESTING DETAIL: The name lepidolite derives from the Greek words *lepidos* and *lythos*, meaning "scale" and "stone" respectively.

FUN FACT: Lithium, the lightest metal in the world, is used in rechargeable batteries, cell phones, various household appliances such as microwave ovens, and aerospace components.

LAPIS LAZULI

- **Mineral family:** cancrinite-sodalite
- **Extraction zones:** Afghanistan, Chile
- **Color:** blue
- **Planet:** Jupiter
- **Sign:** Sagittarius
- **Chakra:** fifth
- **Main purpose:** communication
- **Musical note:** G
- **Body parts affected:** throat, lungs, thyroid gland
- **Keywords:** "Communicate deeply!"

To say "lapis lazuli" is to project oneself into the land of ancient Mesopotamia when the trade of this stone flourished. Intense blue in color with gold-colored specks of pyrite, it reminds us of a bright starry sky.

It works mainly on communicative traits. It connects us with deep feelings, pushing us to transmit them through our most evolved part.

It relaxes the lungs, the organs that symbolically represent freedom. Lapis lazuli expresses its drive on freedom of expression, but also physical movement. It's no coincidence that it's associated with the zodiac sign Sagittarius, the great traveler.

It promotes creativity, especially manual creativity. It encourages research and instills confidence in one's intuition.

Lapis lazuli urges us to diligently search for our wasted gifts. It also asks us to affirm what we deeply desire.

Making people stare reality in the face, it prevents us from hiding from the truth, and thus favors the unfolding of our true essence.

On a physical level, it is effective in strengthening the vocal cords. It is also helpful with colds of the upper airways and in the proper functioning of the thyroid gland.

INTERESTING DETAIL: Lapis lazuli has been used since ancient times by the Sumerians and the Egyptians, who made powerful amulets of protection out of it.

FUN FACT: The ancient Egyptians created jewelry that would accompany the deceased in the tomb, protecting them in the journey to the afterlife.

AQUAMARINE

- **Mineral family:** beryl
- **Extraction zones:** Brazil, Africa, Russia
- **Color:** light blue
- **Planet:** Neptune
- **Sign:** Pisces
- **Chakra:** fifth
- **Main purpose:** farsightedness
- **Musical note:** G
- **Body parts affected:** lungs, myopia
- **Keywords:** "Everything is clearer!"

Aquamarine is known for its intense color, typical of the water element. The influence of this stone is clarity of vision, within us and the outside world.

It exalts our sensitive side, which activates the subtle sight governed by the sixth chakra, the third eye.

It encourages us to regain the enthusiasm we lost after negative experiences and to conquer the joy of flying high to explore the world inside and outside of us. In order to help us overcome obstacles, this stone induces evolutionary but also complex movement to make the problem manifest, and thus deal with it.

It favors the flow of energy taken from the seventh chakra, integrating and dosing it throughout the energy system.

The lungs benefit from it, acquiring greater extension and relieving the constraints and heaviness of the chest or the heart.

Aquamarine is a valuable aid for short-sightedness.

It helps relieve allergies related to bronchi and the lungs, especially in periods of greater pollen spread.

INTERESTING DETAIL: Aquamarine is frequently counterfeited, especially when cut for jewelry. It is important to know that stones with an intense but cold blue color are often the result of a thermal treatment—that is, they have been heated at temperatures around 842°F (450°C) to enhance their color.

FUN FACT: Several years ago, during the pollen season, I accidentally put a large bag of aquamarines near my chest, and after a few minutes I was breathing deeply again like I hadn't in days. What an incredible discovery!

BLUE CHALCEDONY

- **Mineral family:** quartz
- **Extraction zones:** Turkey, Brazil, India
- **Color:** blue
- **Planet:** Jupiter
- **Sign:** Sagittarius
- **Chakra:** fifth
- **Main purpose:** comprehension
- **Musical note:** G
- **Body parts affected:** throat, lungs
- **Keywords:** "Let go!"

Coming across a transparent blue chalcedony is like putting your head underwater and admiring the depths of the sea with its blurred contours.

This variety of quartz precisely transmits the ability of water to flow, especially when we need to come into contact with our emotions, facilitating those tears that have not flowed for a long time and helping, thus, to relieve the emotional pressure that would otherwise cause damage to the inside of our body.

It particularly benefits the quality of communication, to find the right language based on the listeners.

Listening is also enhanced, and it is easier to grasp the nuances that are not normally perceived.

Lungs benefit from it, finding the right expansion, in reference to the symbolism of inner and outer freedom.

Blue chalcedony is an excellent drainer of bodily fluids, especially in the lower limbs. It activates the lymphatic system, which can eliminate the waste of the physical body and more specifically the emotional one.

The throat and upper airways get considerable help in healing from diseases.

INTERESTING DETAIL: The "banded" variety has a crystallization inside that recalls the motion of waves; it is the best type of chalcedony for those who want to work on getting in touch with buried emotions.

FUN FACT: The name comes from the ancient port of Chalcedon in Bithynia, part of the ancient Roman empire in present-day Turkey, where the most beautiful quality crystals are still extracted today.

ANGELITE

- **Mineral family:** calcium sulfate
- **Extraction zones:** USA, Europe
- **Color:** light blue
- **Planet:** Jupiter
- **Sign:** Sagittarius
- **Chakra:** fifth

- **Main purpose:** raising frequencies
- **Musical note:** G
- **Body parts affected:** respiratory system, cerebellum, spinal cord
- **Keyword:** "Calm!"

Angelite influences the subtle and spiritual sphere more than the physical one. Encountering this stone is a very special experience. Its cerulean blue color immediately invokes a feeling of calm.

It exercises its qualities on the communicative level, succeeding in lowering aggressiveness during a discussion.

It amplifies the listening aspect as well as the expression aspect.

It facilitates access to guides and angels; in fact, the name of the stone comes from them. It helps in contacting spirit guides, encouraging communication, and accentuating telepathy between human beings. It therefore does a good job of balancing the physical and subtle body, favoring the communication of data.

It is a stone that tends to increase the vibratory frequencies of the physical and energetic body, thus allowing for good protection from what is considered negative or heavy energy. Wearing angelite offers a peaceful effect that isn't easily undermined by external events.

On a physical level, the cerebellum benefits from angelite, which supports its proper functioning. This stone does a good job on the spinal cord at the intersection of the brain and brain stem.

INTERESTING DETAIL: The name angelite indicates light-blue anhydrite.

FUN FACT: During Reiki and other related practices, angelite accentuates our connection with our intuitive side, which brings out clearer and stronger messages.

AZURITE

- **Mineral family:** carbonate
- **Extraction zones:** Asia, Peru, Madagascar
- **Color:** blue
- **Planet:** Jupiter
- **Sign:** Sagittarius
- **Chakra:** fifth, sixth
- **Main purpose:** clear vision
- **Musical note:** G
- **Body parts affected:** throat, liver, teeth
- **Keywords:** "I speak what I see!"

I think such an intense electric blue is hard to find anywhere else in nature. Azurite is a magnificent stone that affects two different chakras: the fifth and sixth.

Its work on the throat chakra is about communication. Sharp, direct, and absolutely devoid of mediation, azurite pushes us to communicate exactly what we think, regardless of the reactions our ruthless debate might arouse. For this reason, it is recommended to use it on the throat when it's of absolute necessity, carefully considering the time of use.

On the sixth chakra, it performs a unique job in helping us see the subtle reality; in fact, it tends to lift the veils of previous incarnations, allowing us to glimpse our past lives and often helping us to grasp the meaning of the present incarnation in order to identify what we have inherited.

It is a multipurpose stone of great power that must be used sparingly.

It does an excellent job on liver-related diseases, bringing out our aggressive side so it can be used without filters. It is also effective for the teeth, which are directly related to aggressiveness.

INTERESTING DETAIL: Azurite crystals are wonderful, but not easy to find. Azurite often appears in amorphous form or as a rosette.

FUN FACT: In the Middle Ages, it was used as a pigment in frescoes, in substitution of the more expensive ultramarine blue. After many years, however, azurite tended to turn to dust, peeling away from the frescoes, leaving the work bare and the preparation layer visible. What a shame!

SUGILITE
(LUVULITE)

- **Mineral family:** cyclosilicate
- **Extraction zones:** Canada, South Africa, Japan, Italy
- **Color:** purple
- **Planet:** Jupiter
- **Sign:** Sagittarius

- **Chakra:** sixth
- **Main purpose:** clear vision
- **Musical note:** A
- **Body part affected:** nervous system
- **Keywords:** "I am connected!"

Rare sugilite, with its intense purple, offers help to the mechanisms that connect us with the universe. Wearing it, in fact, heightens the senses, expanding them to their maximum potential.

It is a stone that offers help in different ways, depending on our qualities it allows to expand. It pushes the individual to bring out their full potential.

Sugilite allows us to observe ourselves from the inside, finding the gifts that we possess and that, once evolved, will be offered in service through our actions.

It is a stone that very well balances the physical energy with the etheric (the subtlest) energy, integrating them, and allows us to connect to the highest part of the universe, such as the spiritual guides and higher orders.

At the auric level, it is a balm that can restructure the etheric layer and also the emotional one in a good way.

The nervous system, an electrical bridge that connects to the cosmic system, is driven to maximum functioning: everything is ready so that the slightest nuance might be understood.

The blood capillary network is hyperactivated to speed up the exchange of information. The nervous system is also healed.

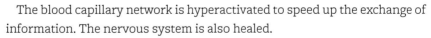

INTERESTING DETAIL: Sugilite is a powerful stimulator of the nervous system; to avoid overload, pay careful attention to how long you use it.

FUN FACT: Meditating while wearing this stone is an experience that can bring good results in terms of lucidity and connection. Try it!

PURPLE FLUORITE

- **Mineral family:** halide
- **Extraction zones:** all over the world; China has remarkable specimens
- **Color:** purple
- **Planet:** Uranus, Saturn
- **Sign:** Aquarius
- **Chakra:** sixth
- **Main purpose:** vision
- **Musical note:** A
- **Body parts affected:** nervous system, intestines, teeth, spinal column, eyes
- **Keywords:** "I welcome!"

Beautiful purple fluorite increases the ability to receive impressions from the physical world and, above all, the spiritual world. It makes you receptive by distinguishing these impressions: those that must be acquired, and those that must be circumvented and avoided.

It contains a strong feminine aspect, which asks us to turn inward to listen to the emotional parts of us that we tend to ignore in our daily lives because they are uncomfortable. It urges us to navigate below the conscious level to explore emotions that, if listened to, could prove to be evolutionary, keys to an important turning point in our lives.

Despite being a violet stone—a color that usually tends to push us from the Earth toward a spiritual connection with the sky—fluorite works on the spiritual side with the intention of helping us turn inward, searching our depths for the spiritual being within us.

It urges the intense processing of the intestines that will both absorb the most important parts and discard waste. The teeth and spine are also fortified by this stone. Purple fluorite also indirectly affects the physical eyes, preventing degeneration of shortsightedness.

INTERESTING DETAIL: Fluorites are unique in that they are multicolored. If you place some specimens in the light, inside them you will see color patterns that range from green to purple, blue to white, and so on, an incredible intertwining of colors.

FUN FACT: Fluorite has different crystal habits, the forms in which it is found in nature. One very fascinating and interesting form is the octahedral one, which is composed of two pyramids, upside down to each other on a shared square base.

AMETRINE
(BOLIVIANITE)

- **Mineral family:** quartz
- **Extraction zones:** Bolivia, Brazil
- **Color:** purple and yellow
- **Planet:** Neptune
- **Sign:** Pisces
- **Chakra:** sixth

- **Main purpose:** balance
- **Musical note:** A
- **Body parts affected:** nervous system, diaphragm, cardia
- **Keyword:** "Stability!"

Ametrine quartz comes from the fusion, or from the heating, of an amethyst which also absorbs the yellow of citrine.

It is an interesting stone for balancing our sensitive side and making it more concrete. The feminine side is supported, rebalanced with the masculine side, which will contain it, rationalize it, and make it less emotional and more lucid. In short, this quartz helps balance male and female energies.

The yellow part of ametrine brings out aspects related to our ego, balancing it so that it can perform great deeds. The balancing of the purple part sparks greater spiritualization: that is, it puts one's work in the service of others and not only for personal purposes.

It brings more rationality where we have an excess of spirituality because this tends to make us perceive things as elusive, creating a sense of frustration in the long term.

On a physical level, it does a good job of relaxing the diaphragm, which provides for the expansion of the lungs.

It helps the cardiac valve, which separates the esophagus from the stomach and opens and closes for the passage of food.

INTERESTING DETAIL: Pay attention when selecting the stone because ametrine is often counterfeit, or artificially created by heating amethyst at high temperatures to make it turn yellow.

FUN FACT: In the seventeenth century, this quartz was brought to Europe by a Spanish colonizer to whom it had been given by the princess of an indigenous population of Bolivia. He received an amethyst stone with two distinct colors from her as a wedding gift, which symbolized the feminine and masculine, the future spouses. It is a very strong stone, not recommended for people who are physically weak and therefore have a poor attitude toward being rooted, as it could cause strong disturbances for them.

WHITE ONYX

- **Mineral family:** chalcedony quartz
- **Extraction zones:** Brazil
- **Color:** white
- **Planet:** Moon
- **Sign:** Cancer
- **Chakra:** seventh

- **Main purpose:** bearer of dense light
- **Musical note:** B
- **Body parts affected:** nervous system, bones, nails
- **Keywords:** "Light on Earth!"

We are accustomed to talking about black onyx, but not many people know about the existence of the white variety. Holding it in your hand, you discover that this stone is lighter than the black variety and semitransparent, and this is indicative of how it acts on the energy system.

It is responsible for bringing light by channeling it from the seventh chakra to the lower chakras, which vibrate at a much slower frequency than the seventh. Its maximum usefulness is expressed on those who have a particularly sensitive, emotional, and spindly physicality and energy structure, which struggles to stay rooted to the ground, and on those who tend to take refuge in the sky to escape from ordinary occupations, closing themselves off in the mental sphere. To this type of person, excessively transparent stones would facilitate the escapism, whereas white onyx brings light and accelerates the frequencies of the lower chakras, pushing them to an inefficient basic functioning. In short, we have by nature a high frequency that can influence not only the spiritual and mental plane but that also brings light to matter, in everyday and denser things.

It is very helpful for those who suffer from the sometimes excessive emotionality of the Earth, and they finally have significant support in dealing with it. White onyx acts indirectly on grounding, and therefore improves the management of practical things, such as money and sexuality. The bone system is fortified.

INTERESTING DETAIL: This stone, because of its color which can often be a light yellow or beige, is often considered low quality and is frequently counterfeited, made of ceramic that obviously has nothing to do with white onyx. Beware when onyx is excessively white, polished to a shine.

FUN FACT: The myth tells that Cupid cut the nails of the sleeping Venus and left them scattered on the floor. All parts of a divine being are immortal, and so the nails were transformed into the stone called onyx, from the Greek *onyx*, nails.

MAGNESITE

- **Mineral family:** calcite
- **Extraction zones:** China, North Korea, Turkey, Russia
- **Color:** white
- **Planet:** Moon
- **Sign:** Cancer

- **Chakra:** seventh
- **Main purpose:** absorption
- **Musical note:** B
- **Body parts affected:** general function, gallbladder, kidneys
- **Keywords:** "I clean!"

Magnesite is used in many ways, some of which are right under our noses. This stone appears as a clustered shape of white color, similar to a pencil eraser at first glance.

As always, the technique of marking (or the ability to recognize the action of natural beings based on their shape) speaks volumes. Magnesite is a kind of eraser that is used on auric bodies to absorb dissonant energies. In particular, it is used at the end of a crystal therapy session to absorb low energy that has moved from the subtle bodies to come to the surface. The auric body will be cleaned like a dirty surface, using only the magnesite.

So it is a stone that tends to push unwanted energy outward, as if it sucked it in and then absorbed it.

In general, it is a good tool for relaxing and stretching muscles. It does an excellent job on the gallbladder and kidneys, significantly decreasing abdominal cramping coming from these two important organs. It also turns out to be excellent for supporting magnesium deficiencies in our body.

INTERESTING DETAIL: Magnesite is dyed to create fake turquoise. To recognize the real turquoise, just make a small incision with a sharp object and check that it is not white under the colored layer; otherwise, it is not turquoise but magnesite.

FUN FACT: Magnesite is used in many different fields. In sports, it is used as a powder for climbing, javelin-throwing, and weightlifting, to absorb sweat and create a better grip; it is also used for aluminum alloys and for production of magnesia (refractory material) in furnaces that reach high temperatures. After China, North Korea has the second-largest mines in the world.

MOONSTONE

- **Mineral family:** feldspar
- **Extraction zones:** Brazil, India
- **Color:** milky white
- **Planet:** Moon
- **Sign:** Cancer
- **Chakra:** seventh

- **Main purpose:** deep feeling
- **Musical note:** B
- **Body parts affected:** female genitals, hormonal system, bones, tendons and muscles of the pelvis
- **Keywords:** "I see!"

Moonstone gets its name from its color, which resembles that of the Moon. It can be placed particularly in two areas of the body: the genitals and the third eye.

It is good to understand the archetype of the moon, that of femininity and sensitivity. It is a stone that is often used for women who have difficulty conceiving. The moonstone helps harmonize the female genital apparatus, especially the ovaries, connecting them and thus favoring pregnancy. We must never forget the holistic view of the body, in which emotions, mind, and spirit are inextricably linked. We must try to use our beloved helpers, the stones, according to the cause and not the symptom, going to the root of the problem and approaching it from the symptoms only in the most critical cases before returning to the cause.

Placed on the third eye, the stone sensitizes intuitiveness and clairvoyance, increasing subtle sight to carry out meditation or healing work.

This crystal brings joy by working on the emergence of one's feminine aspect and acceptance. It can also calm agitation, turning it into a serene lake. It increases seductiveness connected to a balanced femininity.

Moonstone is excellent for the hormonal system. It works well on the elasticity of bones, tendons, and muscles of the pelvis.

INTERESTING DETAIL: Not to be confused with white labradorite, also commercially called moonstone, which is a more transparent white with a blue reflection.

FUN FACT: This stone was originally exposed to the Moon, from which it was thought to absorb its fertile female energy, hence its unique powers.

SELENITE

- **Mineral family:** calcium sulfate
- **Extraction zones:** all over the world, especially in Spain, Tunisia, Morocco
- **Color:** white
- **Planet:** Moon
- **Sign:** Cancer
- **Chakra:** seventh
- **Main purpose:** connection
- **Musical note:** B
- **Body parts affected:** nervous system, long bones of the body
- **Keywords:** "Here is light!"

Selenite owes its name to its resemblance to the Moon, which does a very similar job reflecting light rays and creating fascinating reflections.

Observing this stone, one realizes that they have trapped light in material form in their hands. And it is precisely on light that this stone does its most consistent work, delivering it to human beings.

Humans are formed by a noble part of light and an unresolved part of shadow, and they can use selenite to bring light to the unprocessed part, the unseen side; this will allow them to advance in their evolution, dissolving issues and learning important life lessons.

It is a naturally grooved stone, so it tends to be a fast vehicle of information for the energetic part of the body.

Selenite brings us very close to our divine side, which we will reach by evolving into different incarnations. It almost seems to bring us closer to this part but without allowing us to grasp it, like the donkey-and-carrot mechanism. On the other hand, in the long run selenite will be decisive in pushing human beings to move forward, accepting the challenges of life and continuing to evolve.

To become divine beings, slowly detaching ourselves from the density of human life, is what selenite asks of us.

It does an excellent job on the long bones of the body, and it increases the speed of transmission of the nervous system.

INTERESTING DETAIL: The ancient Greeks, before glass was in common use, created transparent sheets of selenite that let light pass through them and reminded them of the opalescence of the moon.

FUN FACT: In 2002 in Naica, Mexico, an important site of selenite was discovered. When the first speleologists entered, they found crystals that were 50 ft (15 m) high and 6½ ft (2 m) in diameter.

ZODIAC SIGNS AND STONES

Pairing zodiac signs and stones reveals a very important bond that requires the right knowledge of crystal therapy and astrology.

In this book, each stone is paired with a planet and zodiac sign, based on similarity and resemblance. However, it's important to know that the zodiac sign associated with a specific stone does not necessarily draw benefits from that crystal. For example, a Sagittarius connected to purple and blue stones does not automatically receive help from them. The opposite is often true, due to the personality of the individual. If the characteristics of the sign are excessively present in them—as is true for a Sagittarius, already by nature a traveler, who travels too much— then a stone that restores that balance would be better than one that intensifies this aspect.

Whether the zodiac sign is balanced with its principles—there is no deficiency or excess—should be carefully assessed, and only then would it be recommended to wear a stone which will strengthen it, making these character traits more prominent without altering the balance.

CHAPTER 6

HOW TO CHOOSE STONES

There are different ways to identify the right stone for every circumstance. Two rather simple and practical ones are listed below.

Hands

Our hands are very powerful tools of perception. There are varying degrees of sensitivity; and the more we train, the more our hands become a powerful listening tool.

First of all, an important clarification must be made: Not everything that we are attracted to is necessarily good for us. Just think, for example, of the desire we feel toward food that contains chemical or synthetic substances, such as highly refined industrial food. As much as the labels tell us that it is good and healthful, deep down we know that it will not be good for us; but we eat it precisely because we feel its temptation. Bite after bite, our state of health worsens; perhaps not in the immediate future, but in the long run it can cause adverse health effects.

Where does the appeal come from? This kind of food tends to establish and consolidate a typical vicious circle, increasing the problem but also the need that comes from our attraction to the product, which ends up increasing the problem.

This is why a claim that a stone that calls to us is the right one is not always true. The right stone, in fact, should foster a real and profound sense of well-being, acting on the cause and not on the symptom, and even pushing us out of our usual comfort zone when necessary.

Some people naturally enjoy listening to themselves, but we all can cultivate this through exercise in order to distinguish between what is good and what is bad for us.

So, how do we find the right stone? Here are some practical instructions.

- Approach the stone, inhale deeply through your nose and exhale through your mouth, letting go of tension and thoughts.

- Take the stone and hold it in the closed palm of one hand. Listen to the body and try to perceive where it acts. In some areas you will feel insistence, energy, emotions. You will also be able to feel images, smells, and much more, thanks to the senses. Listen to the primary sensation that the stone leaves in your hand. Sometimes you will feel it vibrate or beat. Then listen to your whole body: One or maybe two areas will respond the most. You may feel certain organs being stimulated, feel your heartbeat change, your blood pressure change, feel compression and similar reactions.

Along with the body, the emotions and soul may also respond. You might feel memories surface, visualize colors, see images, and much more. You may experience an immediate reaction related to the problem you want to treat. Depending on what you are looking for, when you feel the stone acting at that point of the body or energy system, you will have identified your helper.

The pendulum

The pendulum is a very interesting tool that allows you to both recognize the most appropriate crystal for a given circumstance, and to determine the correct time of use of the stone. Let me start by saying that to find the necessary answers, you must at least have a basic knowledge of this tool. Let's see how to use it.

Choose the pendulum you are most attracted to. With two fingers, grasp the cord or chain at about two-thirds of the length, letting the shorter end dangle. Sit down and rest your elbow on a table or base of support (make sure the surface is flat and light in color) and then flex your wrist about ninety degrees. Rotate the pendulum broadly clockwise and state deeply: "From now on, this clockwise rotation will concern the answer 'yes' for you." While you rotate the pendulum, repeat this affirmation to yourself for a few minutes, as if it were a mantra, communicating it to your deepest self to internalize it.

Stop the pendulum and gently touch its tip to the floor in order to discharge the information just given; this will allow the pendulum to be ready to store a new request. Now, with a small forward push of the pendulum, ask it to rotate, showing you the movement for the answer "yes." You will see the pendulum begin to rotate with slight jerks of the wrist that are totally out of your control. In the hands of some people, it will move faster and wider, and in other cases, slower and tighter. The width and intensity of the rotation will be different for each person.

At this point, release the information and repeat the same exercise as before, but making the pendulum rotate counterclockwise broadly, and stating clearly: "From now on, this counterclockwise rotation will have to do with the answer 'no' for you."

Always remember to release the information between questions. Now you are ready for the final test.

Place a stone in front of you and ask the pendulum if it is the right stone for you. Next, ask the question in reverse, asking if that is the wrong stone for you. The final result will be correct only when the two answers are different and therefore consistent.

In the case of inconsistent answers, you can perform a relaxation technique that will allow you to clear your mind of thoughts and worries, and then you can repeat the test.

At the beginning, it is frequent to receive wrong answers because it will be your mind controlling the pendulum and not your deeper part. A good exercise to repeat at least ten minutes over several days is a short relaxation technique to stretch your body and loosen your control before doing your pendulum exercises. You will find that working out every day will give you surprising results.

NEGATIVE ENERGY AND ENERGY "VAMPIRES"

———

Over the course of many years of work and study, I have found that people turn to crystal therapy because they have come up with key questions for which they seek answers.

One of these questions concerns the possibility of protecting themselves from the negative energy that they feel surrounds them, energy that generates various kinds of discomfort. It is important to ask ourselves why the negative energy of others might have a certain effect on us. It turns out that we are the greatest producers of negative energy, due to our fears, anxieties, or concerns. These lower the vibration level that fills the physical body, especially the body of energy, with fear hormones. Fear, in fact, releases a series of obsessive and amplified thoughts into the environment, which, over long periods of time, take root in the things that surround us, especially our bed, pillow, and sofa, and thus come back to affect us daily.

Another frequent question is whether there might be people at work or even in our family who seem to suck our energy even simply by standing next to us.

Before recommending a red jasper, the counterquestion always addresses the same issue: Why do these people suck energy from us and not from others? The next (and final) question to ask is: Why are these vampires allowed to suck our energy?

In most cases, finding the right answers and changing our attitude can help overcome the problem without further help.

CHAPTER 7

HOW TO TREAT AND PURIFY STONES

The subject of stone cleansing has always been a matter of deep contradictions. Crystal therapy is an ancient technique. Just think that since the dawn of humanity, crystals were used to make jewelry and amulets for sacred purposes or as common objects (like tools for hunting). Here is a summary of the most effective crystal-cleaning techniques, observed and validated by me, the results of which have been confirmed by both quantitative and qualitative tests.

How stones get dirty

As we have seen, every stone vibrates at a certain frequency. When it is immersed in an environment, it tends to bestow its frequency on the environment in order to reharmonize it. If the environment restores its correct frequency, the crystal can stop acting. If, on the other hand, the environment tends not to rebalance itself, a real conflict will occur. In this process, the stone begins to absorb the altered frequencies of the environment, offering up its own in return. The more the tension persists, the more the crystal absorbs the dysfunctional energy.

Sometimes a stone absorbs so much congested energy that it loses all of its frequency, thus proclaiming the definitive end of its use and, to put it in simpler terms, the crystal dies.

The same thing happens to stones that are worn when heavy energy is clearly prevalent: they end up being overworked. The human being is an elaborate system of energy and emotions; therefore, the stone will have to deal with the management of the different frequencies with which it comes into contact and, if the causes of the heavy energy do not cease, it will suffer.

The death of a stone that is worn is more frequent than one that is exposed to an environment.

Even in this situation, the crystal tends to cease working when the energy center maintains the causes of imbalance. It will continuously attempt to generate the healing frequency, to no effect. If the stone continues to absorb the negative frequency, since the context does not change, the scenario will resemble that of an engine sucking fuel without being able to produce energy.

Recognizing lifeless stones

Recognizing lifeless stones is relatively simple; the quickest way is to observe their brightness and color. If they are dimmed or changed, either partially or significantly, this shows the presence of a problem.

A more thorough method of investigation can be that of the pendulum, which makes it possible to verify whether the crystal is still active or if it is dead.

Cleaning

Certain types of stone can be cleaned with mild soap and water and then rinsed and dried thoroughly. Where it is not possible to use water, a small medium-hard brush can be used to carefully remove dust deposits.

Energetic cleansing

Let's start by saying that stones are not recharged, as we often hear people say, but they must be cleaned of the congested energy they absorb from the environment, which tends to weigh them down and over time can even make them die.

Exposure to the full Moon for three days and very rarely to the Sun helps amplify power that the crystals already possess.

It would be better to avoid the use of materials that are not recyclable or destined to other functions, such as salt (which most of the time damages the stone), exposure to running water at home (in addition to being wasteful, would take days for a proper cleaning, often with damage to the stones themselves), and so on.

Soil

The easiest way to clean stones is to lay them on top of soil. In the city, it is possible to have a garden—or, even more likely, a potted plant. You can also bury the crystal, making sure not to damage the plant. Place the stone at the base of the plant and leave it there for at least seventy-two hours, making sure that the stone is never exposed to direct sunlight, as this can damage the stone, sometimes seriously.

The process happens naturally, as nature has always shown us: think about cultivations irrigated by animal excrement that fertilizes them, favoring the development of new life.

A stone placed in the soil releases the heavy energy it has absorbed to the Earth, and quite simply, the stone expels it while the plant feeds on them.

Dry soil

Some stones can become stained, and others can become damaged by moisture. In the case of stones that suffer from contact with humidity, this cleaning method consists of laying them on the dry soil of a plant for seventy-two hours, away from direct sunlight, placing a natural piece of fabric, such as cotton, between the stone and the Earth, which will prevent direct contact with the Earth, filtering any residual moisture.

Amethyst

The amethyst druse, a set of crystals of this stone, is a suitable surface where we can place our beloved helpers.

Amethyst by nature tends to absorb and transform heavy energy into lighter energy autonomously. It's enough to place the stone on the druse for seventy-two hours away from direct sunlight for significant cleaning.

It is good to know that even the amethyst from time to time should be placed in the ground of a plant to clean it, so that it will let go all the unbalanced frequencies it has absorbed.

HOW TO CLEAN EACH STONE

B elow are the best ways to clean each of the stones included in this book. Remember also that amethyst is the universal way to clean *all* stones.

SOIL

Aquamarine

Amethyst

Ametrine

Green aventurine

Chiastolite andalusite

Carnelian

Red jasper

Garnet

Petrified wood

Black onyx

Black obsidian

Sunstone

Citrine quartz

Hyaline quartz

Rose quartz

Ruby

Emerald

Sodalite

Black tourmaline

DRY SOIL WITH A CLOTH

Blue chalcedony

Orange calcite

Yellow and honey calcite

Yellow fluorite

Purple fluorite

Lapis lazuli

Lepidolite

Malachite

Tiger's eye

White onyx

Moonstone

Pyrite

Rhodochrosite

Sugilite

AMETHYST DRUSE

Angelite

Azurite

Magnesite

Selenite

CHAPTER 8

USAGE TIMES
OF THE STONES

Talking about the usage times of stones is not a simple thing, because each person has a different physicality and thus a subjective type of energy and needs.

There are also stones that should not be worn for prolonged periods of time, and others that lend themselves precisely to this type of use. Crystals that require particularly brief use are indicated within the descriptive cards.

First, remember that crystals are worn only during the day. In the evening, they must be taken off and put away, if possible in a room where you do not sleep; there are stones used at night, but they are specialized for this purpose.

Removing the stones while you rest ensures that they don't further stimulate the physical and energetic body, causing non-restorative sleep, sometimes nightmares or stimulation that doesn't allow for sleep.

Recognizing the right moment to remove a stone is done with the hands and listening. Two situations may occur:

- We no longer feel the stone, and it becomes just another piece of jewelry;

- We feel that after having worn the stone for some time, it begins to cause physical discomfort: for example, it weighs on the neck or creates agitation.

On average, a stone is worn for about fifteen or twenty days, but the duration of its use depends on the person, and careful listening to yourself is recommended.

Determining the usage time of a stone with a pendulum

To determine the usage time of a stone with a pendulum, proceed as follows:

- Place the pendulum about 4 inches (10 centimeters) above the stone.

- Ask for directions regarding the best time to wear it (the method is the same whether it is minutes, hours, or days).

- Wait for a positive response.

For example, in the case of minutes, start counting from 1; when the time is right, the pendulum will move according to the movement identified as affirmative
We can continue similarly with hours or days.

The pendulum is a tool that is particularly easy to influence; therefore, it is always good to ask it a counterquestion, which provides so-called proof of confirmation for the answer we have been given.

For example, if the first time it results that the stone should be worn for fifteen days, you should verify with another question if the stone should be worn for twenty or ten days. If the answer is positive, then the answer was not exact, perhaps because it is influenced by your mind. Then you can make a new request, making sure not to condition the pendulum, perhaps by doing a short relaxation meditation or breathing session first to find your center and the right amount of calm and attention.

INDIRECT USES OF STONES

Crystals are magnificent helpers in ordinary and extraordinary situations for which we never would have imagined using them for our own physical, emotional, and psychological health and that of others.

In the next sections, we will shed light on their main uses.

WATER

Stones can use their vibrations to "inform": in other words, transmit their frequency to other elements that then will become vectors and carriers of it. The element that best accepts their frequency is water. Famous experiments were conducted by the Japanese scientist and researcher Masaru Emoto on the memory of water. When exposed to certain types of classical music, like Schubert's *Ave Maria* or the sound of kind words like "thanks" and "I love you" and then frozen, water forms harmonic crystals. If, however, the water is exposed to rude words and expressions like "I hate you" and "die" or heavy metal music, the frozen water produces irregular, almost broken crystals: likewise with water simply taken from a very polluted place.

It's important to remember that living beings are largely composed of water, which holds information that comes from thoughts and what's said or heard. This could be illuminating for how we face different areas of life based on the surrounding vibrations and the effects they have.

According to studies by Dr. Emoto, having water you will drink touch a leaf inscribed with words like "love," "kindness," and "forgiveness" will ensure that information reaches deep into the molecules and thus the cells of the receiver, transmitting positive or negative messages depending on where they started.

LOTIONS

If rose quartz is dropped in body lotion for at least a night, its beneficial frequencies will pass to the water in the lotion, which draws information from the crystal and acts by hydrating the skin and generating truly remarkable end results.

You can also substitute the rose quartz with another stone based on your needs at the moment. Putting a citrine in lotion before using it to massage the solar plexus can help increase self-esteem or bring out the courage we might need. We must then identify our favorite stones and make a so-called compress with lotion. We can obtain significant advantages without having to use crystals directly.

An important point is to consider the sensitivity of the stones to water. For compresses, it's always best to use ones that don't fear it so that you don't damage the stone and avoid residue in the lotion that would then scratch the skin during the massage. To that end, it's best to use polished stones that are energetically and physically clean or, whenever possible, rough crystals like hyaline quartz.

ELIXIRS

Just like lotions, it's possible to "infuse" stones to obtain a very deep harmonization of the cells.

It's important to know that during the extraction and semi-processing phases of the stones, they are often bonded with oils and industrial substances that can be damaging to our health. Therefore, it's important to avoid the direct use of stones in water.

Just use a pitcher or glass jar as an inactive material. By placing the crystal in contact with the *external* surface of the container, the information from the stone will pass through it and directly into the water, avoiding the possible damaging substances of the crystal. Just make sure the stone stays in direct contact with the glass for at least three consecutive hours, but do not exaggerate with daily consumption of the elixir, which should reach its full potential with two-thirds of a glass of water. This might seem like a small amount, but it will be committed to memory in a very powerful way on a deeper level. Exaggerating with water could cause the body, out of protection, to block absorption of the frequency or produce strong reactions in the physical, emotional, mental, and spiritual realms.

Before using, clean the stones physically and energetically, using one of the techniques mentioned in this book.

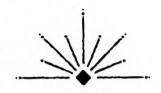

PHOTO
CATALOG

THE 9 MAIN STONES

Amethyst

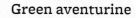

Green aventurine

Carnelian

Red jasper

Black onyx

Citrine quartz

Hyaline quartz
(or rock crystal)

Rose quartz

Sodalite

LESSER STONES

Aquamarine

Ametrine

Angelite

Azurite

Blue chalcedony

Orange calcite

Yellow and honey
calcite

Chiastolite andalusite

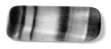

Yellow fluorite

Purple fluorite

Garnet

Lapis lazuli

Petrified wood

Lepidolite

Magnesite

Malachite

Tiger's eye

White onyx

Black obsidian

Moonstone

Sunstone

Pyrite

Rhodochrosite

Ruby

Selenite

Emerald

Sugilite

Black tourmaline

THE PENDULUM

LUCA APICELLA

....

Since childhood, Luca has been attracted to nature and the energy that comes from the Earth. This call led him to study Reiki, starting a wonderful journey that would introduce him to naturopathy and bionatural healing. Over the years, he has added crystal therapy and other energy disciplines to his list of competencies, his work tools, and the subject of his teaching and education. Since 2021, he has been an expert facilitator in forest medicine (shinrin-yoku) and counselor in psychosomatic therapy.

In his in-person and online courses, he combines his training with being in nature and forests, knowing that coming into contact with our beloved trees and nature from which we come can make a difference over a short period of time.

ALESSANDRA DE CRISTOFARO

....

Alessandra is an illustrator for magazines, communication agencies, and international publishing houses. Her work is inspired by her holistic and spiritual interests and is marked by her focus on the relationship between the interior and exterior worlds, which is expressed through a dreamlike and surreal atmosphere, developed from a "pop" perspective.